EYE
EARS THAT HEAR

EYES THAT SEE, EARS THAT HEAR

PERCEIVING JESUS IN A POSTMODERN CONTEXT

JAMES P. DANAHER, PhD

Liguori/Triumph
LIGUORI, MISSOURI

Imprimi Potest:
Thomas D. Picton, C.Ss.R.
Provincial, Denver Province
The Redemptorists

Published by Liguori/Triumph
An imprint of Liguori Publications
Liguori, Missouri
www.liguori.org

Library of Congress Cataloging-in-Publication Data

Danaher, James P.
    Eyes that see, ears that hear : perceiving Jesus in a postmodern context / James P. Danaher.
        p. cm.
    Includes bibliographical references and index.
    ISBN-13: 978-0-7648-1409-9 ; ISBN-10: 0-7648-1409-5
    1. Jesus Christ—Person and offices. 2. Postmodernism—Religious aspects—Christianity. I. Title.
BT203.D36 2006
230'.046—dc22   2006029018

Liguori Publications, a nonprofit corporation, is an apostolate of the Redemptorists. To learn more about the Redemptorists, visit *Redemptorists.com.*

Printed in the United States of America
10 09 08 07 06   5 4 3 2 1
First edition

For my brother, Kevin Danaher

Contents

Preface

Our perception of reality is certainly changing. We are rapidly moving beyond the modern world to which we had become so accustomed over the last three hundred years. What is the blessing that God has for us in these changes? God always has a blessing, if we have eyes to see and ears that hear (see Romans 11:8). So how are we to perceive this changing world in order that we do not miss God's blessing?

Many have dubbed this new world *postmodern*. Of course, no one seems to be able to say exactly what that means. In fact, any attempt at a definition would be premature and presumptuous. The situation appears to be very much like a similar transition in worldview that took place during the seventeenth century. By the year 1650, René Descartes (1596–1650) and Francis Bacon (1561–1626) had already published new views concerning how we should understand our world. As these new views spread, the medieval world was passing away, but in 1650 Isaac Newton (1642–1727) was only eight years old, and it would be a while before the scientific and philosophical perspectives of the modern world would take shape. It seems that a similar situation exists today. The modern world, whose meta-narrative was that of Enlightenment science, is passing away, but we are not yet able to define the precise nature of the new, postmodern worldview into which we are so rapidly moving. At this point, the most that can be said about our present state is that it is marked by a general rejection of modernity. In fact, postmodernism is, at present, best defined by its suspicion of modernity and its ideals.

Modernity refers to the Enlightenment of the seventeenth and eighteenth centuries. The cornerstone of the Enlightenment was a belief in a new and *enlightened* form of science. This science maintained that not only was the world orderly, but that such an order was governed by mathematically precise laws that could be detected by the new science. Thus a precise and certain understanding of the world, in time, became the great meta-narrative and model for all right thinking. According to the Enlightenment, as this new science acquired more and more knowledge, it would eventually bring us to utopia.

Of course, from the start, the Enlightenment had its critics. The end of Enlightenment science as the great meta-narrative, however, was not brought about by the criticism of poets and philosophers, but rather by the events of the twentieth century. After three hundred years of putting our faith in scientific progress, the twentieth century never became the utopia that modernity had promised. Quite the contrary—the twentieth century witnessed more than 100 million people killed in wars, and 35,000 to 40,000 children dying each day from the effects of hunger and malnutrition. By the end of the century, the very existence of the planet's biosphere was being threatened, and science seemed unable to do anything about it. The Enlightenment had failed to deliver what it had promised, and something else was obviously needed. This lacuna presents a great opportunity for the gospel.

Not only are people searching for answers today in a way that they hadn't when science still appeared to hold all the answers, but, with the end of modernity, we no longer believe that knowledge must be objective and mathematically or scientifically precise. Thus, there is room for the kind of knowledge of which the gospel speaks. A Christian understanding of God will always be based on a personal relationship with the risen Christ, and never the kind of objective and precise understanding upon which modernity insisted. The Christian God could never be discovered through the methods of science, but he faithfully reveals himself to those who humbly seek him.

The Enlightenment gave us the science and technology that runs our contemporary society, but it is not capable of leading us to the kind of truth and meaning that lie at the base of Christian life. It certainly is not an appropriate model for intimately knowing a personal God, for it tells us that we should rid ourselves of all bias in order to discover an objective truth untainted by our own prejudice. The gospel, however, tells us that we are to bring the prejudice of faith to every circumstance. Modernity provided us with a method that gave us a confidence in our certain and precise understanding, but the gospel leads us to an understanding founded upon a divine beauty that we behold in humble awe. The objective and mathematically precise truths of modernity were truths that we could get a hold of, but the truth of the gospel is something that gets a hold of us, changes us, and forms us into more loving and forgiving beings.

Fortunately, we now know that the scientific reasoning that modernity insisted upon is not the universal form of right reason it had claimed to be but merely represents one form of reason. With that understanding, we are now free to pursue forms of rationality more compatible with a gospel that is personal and mysteriously beautiful rather than objective and mathematically precise.

Contrary to what some have led us to believe, a postmodern world is not one in which all order, meaning, and truth is lost. Rather, all that is lost is the kind of order, meaning, and truth that modernity had insisted upon. The good news of the postmodern gospel is that, with the end of modernity, we now have an ever-greater opportunity to order our lives, not based on an understanding of some universal, objective truth, but rather on an intimate understanding of a truth that is personal—indeed, a truth that is a person (see John 14:6).

JAMES P. DANAHER
NYACK COLLEGE
NYACK, NEW YORK

Introduction

Having reached the twenty-first century, we now know that the concepts that lie at the base of our understanding are not God-given as we had once believed. Even if some of our concepts are innate, or the result of mental hardware that produces certain universal concepts, most are the product of human conventions at work within culture and history. This new understanding of the human condition is one in which our all-too-human concepts filter our experience and keep us from knowing things as they are in themselves. Although the science of modernity told us that we should be able to seek an objective understanding of the world that is free of all prejudice or bias, we now know that such an understanding is beyond our human reach.

From the postmodern perspective, our concepts of things such as law, sin, love, and faith are not God-given but inherited from our language communities and cultures. Since we interpret the gospel in the light of these concepts inherited from language and culture, we create for ourselves a tribal Jesus who reflects our cultural and historical background.

Many people view this postmodern insight as a threat to Christianity. They believe that if we can no longer rely on language to reflect objective reality, our basis for truth, particularly the truth of the gospel, will be lost. Because of this, many Christians, despite all the evidence to the contrary, try to defend some type of linguistic realism at all costs. In actuality, however, the postmodern condition, which might undermine truth as modernity understood it, is actually much more conducive to bringing us into the truth of the gospel.

This is the central thesis of this text: There is good news in the fact that our understanding is perspectival (coming from a particular, unique perspective)—that is, the result of the cultural milieu that comprises our experience. Since we are now aware that the perspective through which we experience the world is not God-given, we are free, as never before, to rethink the concepts that lie at the base of our understanding in ways that might allow us to come more fully into that life to which Jesus calls us.

One reason that many of us are not changed by what we find in the gospels is that we read the words of Jesus without being aware of the culturally relative and conventional nature of our own conceptual understanding through which we interpret those words. We assume a naive realism and imagine that God has somehow equipped us with the ability to form correct concepts that reflect or mirror reality as God created it. Thus we do not appreciate how radically different Jesus' concepts were. We falsely assume that the Jesus of history must have had the same essential concepts that we have today.

The emerging twenty-first century mindset allows us to approach the Scriptures with a postmodern suspicion concerning our own concepts. This suspicion, along with a willingness to allow our concepts to be changed, opens us to the possibility of being transformed by what we find in the gospels. Without such a suspicion we will forever make Jesus into our likeness rather than being made more into his likeness.

Of course, there are those who think that, despite the fact that our concepts are the product of sociohistorical forces and therefore different from Jesus' own concepts, we can discover the meaning of Jesus' words through a rigorous study of the language and culture of his day. This would be true if Jesus' concepts were the product of the world in which he lived. Many of Jesus' key concepts, however, seem to have been radically different from the concepts that were common to his world. In fact, much of the conflict Jesus had with the religious leaders of his day, and what ultimately led to his death, resulted from the fact that his concepts were so radically different from those of his day.

Consider, for example, Jesus' concept of law. One of the charges continually leveled against Jesus was that he was undermining the law of God. Of course, Jesus claimed that he was not undermining the law but rather fulfilling it (see Matthew 5:17–18). Obviously, Jesus had a very different concept of law than those who saw him as a threat to that law. Even more blasphemous was his concept of God. Not only did

Jesus maintain that God was his own Father, but he claimed that God was our Father as well (see Matthew 5:16, 5:45, 5:48, 6:1–18, 7:11, 10:20, 10:29, 18:14, 23:9; Mark 11:25; Luke 6:36, 12:30; and John 20:17). To conceptualize the God of the universe as "our Father" was perceived as demeaning the greatness of God. Such a notion was certainly very different from who the religious people of Jesus' day imagined God to be. Of course, there were Old Testament Scriptures that could have led us to believe that we were God's beloved sons and daughters, but no one seemed able to comprehend this fully until Jesus. Until Jesus, no one brought that perspective to their everyday experience.

In addition to his radical understanding of his relationship to God and the law, Jesus also offered radically new concepts of sin, righteousness, love, faith, good, and evil. Like other great historical figures, many of Jesus' concepts were unique to his own experience and understanding. Unlike so many others, however, Jesus never wrote long texts explaining the concepts that made up his unique perspective. Thus, while we have come to realize the relative nature of our own conceptual understanding, we cannot achieve Jesus' understanding simply by knowing the cultural and historical concepts of his day. In fact, it may be impossible to discover the precise understanding that Jesus personally attributed to those concepts that lay at the base of his unique perspective. We can, however, rethink some of the more basic concepts that lie at the base of our understanding, and which constitute our perspective of the gospel, in ways that would allow us to come more fully into the life promised by Jesus. In short, we need to change the concepts through which we perceive the gospel.

There was a time when people saw the sun go around the earth and the stars move across the heavens. They saw this because they had wrong concepts through which to understand what they saw. Copernicus offered new concepts and thus a new perspective. He claimed that it was the earth's rotation that made it look like the sun was going around the earth, and it was not the stars that were moving but the earth. The church of his day claimed that Copernicus was wrong, because our eyes tell us that the sun goes around the earth and that the stars move and not the earth. Of course, Copernicus was right, and it is not simply our eyes that tell us how the heavens move, but rather the concepts that constitute our perspective. Eventually, we were able to change our perspective concerning such things, but are we able to change our perspective of the

3

gospel in ways that will bring us into the ever-greater fullness of life that Jesus promises?

The Nature of Our Understanding

Our experience is always perspectival and filtered through concepts that are relative to cultures, historical epochs, and philosophies. This is as true concerning our experience of a text as it is concerning our experience of the world. It is, however, possible for our concepts to change, and to change specifically because of what we encounter in a text or experience in the world. The biblical text is no exception. Indeed, the possibility for change is heightened in biblical text since the Holy Spirit works to renew our minds as we open ourselves to the text. Of course, in order for our concepts to change because of what the Spirit reveals in the biblical text, we must approach the text with the postmodern suspicion that we do not possess correct concepts. If we hold the view that we do indeed possess correct concepts, the text will always conform to those concepts rather than our concepts conforming to the text, and thus the power of the Spirit to renew our mind will be stifled. In order to be changed, our conceptual perspective must be open to change.

Unfortunately, many cling to the sacredness of their own concepts rather than the sacredness of the biblical text, and such people see no need for the Spirit to renew their conceptual understanding. For them, the text does little more than confirm their prejudicial perspective. Fortunately, such a belief is no longer as easily maintained as in the past. Today, even if we believe that we are equipped with some innate hardware that allows us to form predetermined concepts, that same hardware also appears to allow us the liberty to modify or alter our concepts. In other words, even if our "wiring" is God-given, our thought process is free to form unique concepts.

Postmodernism has emerged through a variety of historical, political, social, scientific, theological, and philosophical influences, but its primary themes can be traced to several theoretical shifts. For example, during the eighteenth century Immanuel Kant (1724–1804) proposed that what we bring to experience and what filters that experience is a universal hardware, or way of reasoning. The structure of that innate reason determines our experience of objects. During the nineteenth century, however, others proposed that this conceptual filter was not as innate or universal as proposed by Kant. Rather, our conceptual framework was considered to be relative to socially constructed concepts inherited from our respective language communities and cultures. By the twentieth century, Ludwig Wittgenstein (1889–1951) showed us that much of what we had thought were metaphysical problems, or part of the reality of the external world, were actually problems of language and thus traceable to the reality of our culture and communication environments. Other theorists—particularly the structuralists and poststructuralists—of the twentieth century made us aware of the fact that words have their meaning, not because of their reference to things, but because of their reference to concepts. These concepts, they claim, derive much of their meaning from their relationship to other concepts. The consequence of this is that our understanding of one concept is affected by our understanding of another concept. Because so many of these concepts are intertwined, and since they all affect one another, every mind could be perceived as a singularly unique web of understanding. Like human fingerprints, no two human concepts are alike—even if they may appear similar from a distance.

Additionally, by the second half of the twentieth century, Thomas Kuhn (1922–1996) made us aware of the fact that our understanding of the world is always based on paradigms or narrative models that further filter and mold our understanding.

These theoretical models are not, and cannot be, chosen by some objective criteria but are based on some cultural agenda. Aristotle, for example, imagined that the world was biological. Such a paradigm was coherent in that it was consistent with the rest of Aristotelian thought, but it also gave Aristotle and those who followed him the kind of understanding they desired. By contrast, Isaac Newton's paradigm was that of a machine because it gave him and his followers the kind of understanding they desired. Newton's paradigm of the world as a machine provides a better model by which to pursue technological progress than did Aristotle's biological paradigm. Of course, if our interest is ecology rather than technological progress, it may be best to conceive of the world according to a biological model.

Since such paradigms cannot find a rational ground in observation, but instead are based in some overarching agenda, we need to be aware of the agenda(s) that so greatly affect our understanding. Michel Foucault

(1926–1984)—one of the fathers of postmodernism—spent much of his time clarifying that many of the paradigms inherited from our language communities and cultures were originally selected by the powerful because they served their interests and not because they best represented some objective reality. Of course, most of us are unaware of the agendas behind these paradigms and merely accept them as cultural norms. Once accepted, we then naively suppose that they represent something "real." This is the case with almost all of our concepts. They come to us through language acquisition and acculturation, but we remain oblivious to the agendas and philosophies at their bases. The common notion is that philosophy is something we reach at the pinnacle of our thinking. However, in fact, philosophy is at the very base of our thinking, even if it is sometimes unexamined.

Considering all these facts, that which we had previously believed to be our objective understanding of the world begins to deconstruct, we realize that the nature of language does not allow our understanding to be a perfect reflection of reality. That, however, does not mean that language breaks down and communication becomes impossible. What has broken down is the belief that human beings can reach some objective reality that is unaffected by language and our perspectival understanding. What deconstructs is our idea that human language, and thus our understanding which is cast in language, are based on an identity between words and objective reality. In truth, words in general refer to concepts within our understanding and thus one can never escape the understanding in order to get to some "thing" in itself.

The great revelation of our day is that the world, as we know it, is always filtered. We do not have access to a neutral or objective understanding of the world, and all we can ever know is a phenomenal reality—or reality as we perceive it—through the conceptual grid of our understanding. The reality into which God has been pleased to place us is not a noumenal reality whereby we experience things as they are in themselves. Rather God has placed us in a reality through which we experience things as they appear in a human perspective that has been molded by a host of cultural, historical, and philosophical concepts. Furthermore, just as our understanding of the world is phenomenal rather than objective, so, too, is our understanding of God. Our theology will always be a phenomenal theology, and it can only reveal a human perspective of God.

Of course, in the past, our ancestors were unaware of all the filters that we now know exist. It was much easier for many of them to maintain a belief that we possessed something like an objective knowledge of both the world and God. For such realist ancestors, human understanding was, for the most part, objective and universal rather than unique to historical periods, cultures, or individual perspectives. Many today bemoan the loss of such an objective and universal view of the world. They reason that if we are not able to know an ultimate, objective reality, we are not able to know God, since God is the ultimate, objective reality. This, however, is a mistake. It may have been Plato's and Aristotle's ambition to know an ultimate objective reality, but it should never have been the ambition of anyone who wishes to follow Jesus. In order to follow Jesus, we should not seek some objective reality, but a correct perspective through which to understand and interpret our experience and relationship with the personal God that he reveals.

Human language may not be capable of achieving objective reality, but it is well suited to communicate our unique conceptualizations to one another. Language is still very much suited for that purpose. Although Jacques Derrida (famous French literary critic and philosopher, 1930–2004)—another father of postmodernism—may claim that language is not suited to accurately describe the world as we had traditionally supposed it to be, that does not prevent him, or anyone else, from communicating his unique conceptual understanding. When I read Derrida, I am convinced that language cannot reflect or mirror objective reality, but I am also convinced that language is able to allow Derrida to communicate his unique perspective. For the purpose of communicating a unique personal understanding, language is still intact. In fact, it is better than ever since we are now sensitive to difficulties in communication that went unnoticed in the past. We now know, as never before, that if we want to intimately know another person, there is a uniqueness to their understanding that we must grasp. In the past, this uniqueness was not so obvious. Since much of our understanding is shared because of language acquisition and education, it was assumed that our understanding was common and universal. Today that innocence has been lost, and we now realize that people often have very different conceptual understandings. Such differences, however, can be communicated as long as we begin by acknowledging their potential.

Contemporary insights are enormously beneficial in attempting to know another person, especially the person of Jesus. In attempting to know and follow Jesus, it is essential that we understand that he is not attempting to communicate some objective reality, but rather his unique conceptualization of God and who we are in relationship to God. Jesus does not give us knowledge of God's objective identity, but rather a correct perspective or understanding from which to interpret *our* God experiences. In order to know and follow Jesus, we need to have his perspective and discover God in a similar way. We need to bring to our every experience the perspective and understanding that Jesus brought to his experiences. We do not seek knowledge of God's objective identity (we cannot know it); rather we seek the correct perspective that God desires us to have concerning our relationship with him.

The Problem of Knowing God

The God that Jesus reveals is a subject and not an object, and just as we can never completely and objectively know any human subject, God can never be ultimately and objectively known by human beings. Additionally, since God is divine, our understanding will necessarily be even more limited than it would be with human persons. As a consequence, any theology that attempts to be precise and systematic is a fiction because it attempts to reduce an infinite God to the realm of human understanding. Karl Barth (1886–1968) puts it best when he says:

> My lectures at the University of Basel are on "Systematic Theology." In Basel and elsewhere the juxtaposition of this noun and this adjective is based on a tradition which is quite recent and highly problematic. Is not the term "Systematic Theology" as paradoxical as "wooden iron"? One day this concept will disappear just as suddenly as it has come into being.[1]

Of course, in order to have a relationship with God, we must attempt some sort of understanding, but such understanding must be personal rather than systematic. If we understand that the kind of knowledge we seek is that of a person, we are in a position to understand better the revelations Jesus offers.

The matter is complicated by the fact that the divine subject whom we seek to know is, in many ways, radically different from anything human. Certainly God's thoughts are not our thoughts (see Isaiah 55:8–9). A God's-eye view is a view from eternity and out of our reach. What is not out of our reach, however—and what is quite possible—is that we gain insight into the perspective that God desires us to have so that we might come into the fullness of life that God offers. In order to do so, we must begin by humbly admitting our ignorance in a way that would allow our conceptual understanding to be changed by the Spirit and the biblical text.

Consequently, the contemporary insight that our concepts are not sacred or God-given is the very thing that allows the Spirit and the biblical text to take on a power they do not have over those who imagine that they possess right concepts. People who come to the text with what they consider to be correct concepts of such things as forgiveness, sin, faith, and love will insist that they know what the text means, just as people who believed they had correct, God-given concepts insisted when they saw the sun go around the earth. Those who, on the other hand, acknowledge that their concepts are less than divine are open to the possibility of changes in their conceptual understanding that are more compatible with the spirit of the gospel.

The Method

The method by which our concepts are changed is not the kind of method that might be readily acceptable to the reader who is still under the spell of modernity. One of the maxims at the root of modern, scientific thinking was that we are not to believe anything without sufficient evidence. This was a moral obligation for the modern thinker, who would insist that whatever concepts we propose would be supported by scientific evidence. But what would such scientific evidence look like? Followers of modernity would perhaps want us to link the concepts we propose to the cultural and linguistic concepts of Jesus' day. Understand what the words of Jesus meant in his culture and language community and you will understand his message. Unfortunately, as mentioned previously, the key concepts of many innovative thinkers—including Jesus—are different from those of their culture and language communities. As we have said, Jesus' problems with the Pharisees and Sadducees might be seen as largely the result of his very different concepts. Of course, if Jesus had concepts very different from his language community and culture, and he never wrote long treatises explaining what he meant by sin, love, or faith, how could we claim to know such concepts, and what would serve as evidence for our claim?

If whatever speculations we offer must be supported by the kind of evidence that the science of modernity demands, we are in a hopeless situation. Demanding evidence for all the concepts we propose, however, is irrational because such a demand forces us to fall back on our own inherited, cultural concepts, which are themselves without evidential support. Furthermore, our own cultural concepts on which we fall back are almost certainly different from Jesus' own concepts and, in many ways, antithetical to the spirit of the gospel. Thus, the seventeenth- and eighteenth-century, modern, scientific mentality—which, incidentally, most people still accept today—forces us to receive a gospel that is hopelessly relative to our own culture.

It seems that a postmodern approach, which would allow us to accept concepts that are more compatible with the gospel and more conducive to bringing us into the fullness of the Christian life, would be more "reasonable." Such concepts would, of course, be supported by evidence, but it would be the kind of evidence of which Jesus spoke. That is, Jesus told us that it is by a thing's fruit that it is known (see Matthew 7:17–19, 12:33, 13:23; Mark 4:20; Luke 6:43–44, 8:14–15; and John 12:24, 15:2–16). Therefore, if a certain concept is more fruitful than our cultural concept and able to bring us into a greater fullness of the Christian life, why should we not accept that concept? This seems to be the only key that would allow us to know the difference between our cultural concepts and those God would desire us to have.

We will never know if our concepts exactly replicate Jesus' own concepts. Indeed, even if we would, by chance, stumble upon a concept that closely resembles an exact concept of Jesus, we would have no way of knowing that we had achieved such a replication. What is possible, however, is that we reconstruct the essential concepts that lie at the base of our understanding in ways that allow us to better follow Jesus and come more fully into the life that God has for us.

This book attempts to do just that.[2] The first chapter compares the modern notion of truth with the postmodern concept of truth. The point is to show that the postmodern concept of truth is more compatible with the gospel and more conducive to bringing us into the fullness of the Christian life.

We then proceed to the concept of faith (chapter 2) and the long-standing debate over whether faith is emotive or cognitive. When we examine the gospels, however, we see that faith is not only both emotive and cognitive but ultimately takes other forms as well—indeed, forms that do not look at all like what we generally consider faith to be.

The third chapter discusses three important ways in which love, as it is revealed in Scripture, is radically different from love as we normally perceive it. The most important of these differences is that human love is narrow and directed toward the good or the beautiful, and divine love, as Jesus reveals it, is broad and extends even to those who are neither good nor beautiful in our sight but who are precious to God.

Like faith and love, our concept of sin is more the product of our culture rather than a reflection of what Jesus says. Thus in chapter 4 we consider what Jesus says in the Sermon on the Mount and elsewhere in order to derive a very different perspective from the normative view. Most of us think of sin and evil as synonymous. Based on what Jesus says, however, the implication seems to be that evil is something very different from sin. Evil seems to be the destruction that follows from sin rather than being synonymous with sin. Likewise, our idea of the good seems to be equally lacking, so in chapter 5 we attempt a better understanding of good and evil. We all think we know what is good but this, too, is more a cultural prejudice and we would do well, as Christians, to take a more suspicious view of our idea of the good.

The fact that our understanding is perspectival and all-too-human is especially true concerning our concept of law—as described in chapter 6. If we receive our concept of law from authoritarian parents or from a society intent upon order, we will have a very different concept than one who has a loving parent and whose dictates are intended as blessings. It appears that Jesus must have received his concept of law from a loving Father who promises that if we walk in his presence, we will not murder or steal, lie, or commit adultery. In order to understand Jesus' gospel, we need to understand law as the promises of a loving

Father, and not the commandments of an authoritarian god intent upon strict order.

Following the chapter on law, we consider our ideas of atonement and forgiveness (chapter 7). After a brief look at three traditional theories of atonement, an alternative view of atonement as pure forgiveness is offered. The main point of the chapter, however, is to further set the stage for a postmodern reading of the gospel—that is, a reading that does not offer a fixed and certain definitive understanding, but rather an ever-greater personal insight into the nature of God.

The next two chapters (8 and 9) deal with our concepts of divine and human identity. These concepts are connected to even deeper concepts of substance and relation. From our all-too-human perspective, we imagine that God's identity is substantive rather than relational. Jesus seems to indicate that the reverse is the case, and God is ultimately relational rather than substantive. Like our understanding of the divine identity, our understanding of human identity is also perspectival and relative to cultural and historical factors. As we imagine the divine identity to be substantive, we imagine our own human identity to be substantive as well. The gospel, however, is capable of creating a very different perspective, if only we would allow it.

Chapter 10 addresses salvation. As with our other concepts, salvation is also ill-conceived and very different from what we find in the gospels. Our concept of salvation is usually understood as a matter of being saved from hell. It may be quite natural for us to expect God to be the great punisher of disobedience because that is what we have come to expect from our experience with human authority. Jesus, however, gives us a very different picture of salvation.

Similarly, our cultural concepts of truth and beauty (chapter 11) are also very different from those found in the gospels. These differences relate to the science of modernity, which has so greatly affected our thinking, elevated truth, and marginalized beauty. The gospel, however, offers us a very different picture. Indeed, it is in fact beauty that is more at the core of the gospel, and that beauty generally precedes and has a more central role in the Christian life than truth.

As a final concept (chapter 12), we examine our idea of happiness. We all desire happiness, but few of us find it. Indeed, few of us can even define it. Happiness, as a cultural concept, has very little meaning apart from some vague notion of pleasure or contentment. There is, however, a concept of happiness that is more compatible with the gospel.

In the concluding chapter of the text, we take a deeper look into the nature of concepts in general and how they are communicated.

1

Truth: A Modern and Postmodern View

M any people of faith perceive the emergent, postmodern world as a threat to their faith. They incorrectly assume that in a postmodern world there are no absolute truths, which they take to mean that there is no God. There are, however, many postmodern Christians who claim that we should employ a postmodern skepticism or suspicion, not about the existence of an absolute truth (such as God), but about our access to that truth.

> It seems to me that the postmodern arguments are about the limits of human understanding and that they support the claim that we do not have access to the Truth. But that is different from the claim that there is no Truth, which would be true only if there were no other subject or subjects capable of Truth.[1]

Postmodern Christians do not maintain that they have no access to the truth, but merely that they do not have the kind of access to the truth that modernity had set forth as its model. Since postmodernism has yet to take its final form, at this point, the only characteristic that unites a vast variety of people who consider themselves postmodern is that they reject many of the principles upon which modernity was founded. Even today's science, which has rejected many Enlightenment (modernist) beliefs and attitudes, is being referred to by some as *postmodern* to distinguish it from modern, Enlightenment science. Modern, Enlightenment science equated knowledge with demonstrable certainty. Today, science concedes "that knowledge as a human endeavor, though never certain, can be overwhelmingly probable."[2]

Despite the fact that contemporary science rejects modernist certitude, many Christians still embrace modernist thinking. These contemporary modernists continue to embrace a theology that equates knowledge with certainty. History has revealed that these modern theologies influenced the ideology that fueled the religious wars of the modern period, as well as the schisms that produced scores of Christian denominations. Today such thinking continues to be found at the base of Christian fundamentalism.

If the postmodern critique of modernity does nothing else, we should be thankful that it has made many of us aware that God knows the truth in a way that human beings do not. This postmodern suspicion does not concern the existence of an absolute truth but rather a suspicion concerning the nature and extent of our access to such truth. Of course, the postmodernist who is not a believer may simply claim that there is no absolute truth, but that is not the position of the postmodern Christian.

The Modern Quest for Truth

The modernist notion of truth, and our understanding of it, was shaped by several influential thinkers in the early modern period. For example, Francis Bacon and John Locke (1632–1704) stressed the empirical nature of what would become the modern scientific mind, while Isaac Newton (1642–1727) and Gottfried Wilhelm Leibniz (1646–1716) introduced the integral calculus, thereby allowing us to analyze moving objects with respect to mathematics. Newton's other contribution to modernity was his mechanical view of the universe. This concept overturned the ancient biological paradigm. Aristotle (384–322 BCE) understood the world biologically rather than mechanically, and Plato (427–347 BCE), in the *Timaeus*, says that the world has a soul and is a living thing. By contrast, Newton's mechanical approach did not interpret the world as an organic or transcendental being, but as a machine that operated according to demonstrable laws. Perhaps even the human brain could be charted with the precision by which we chart the stars. Or the truths of religion could be analyzed with scientific rigor. Newton, Leibniz, and their peers initiated a quest for more clarity in all the sciences (including philosophy and theology). As great as their influence was, however, even more basic to the formation of modernist thinking was the influence of René Descartes (1596–1650). His method of inquiry—known appropriately as the Cartesian method—revolutionized the way the world thought about truth and our knowledge of it.

René Descartes

In his *Discourse on Method*, Descartes outlines a method of reasoning that would drastically shape the thinking of the modern period. The purpose of his method was to establish foundations for human knowledge that were based in truths that were as certain as the truths of mathematics—which was held to be the most superior method of reasoning. Mathematics, claimed Descartes, began by accepting "nothing as true which [was] ... not clearly recognized to be so."[3] According to Descartes:

> [we should] avoid...any prejudice in judgments, to accept in them nothing more than what was presented to [the] mind so clearly and distinctly that [we] could have no occasion to doubt it.[4]

Of course, by attempting to eliminate "any prejudice," Descartes was inadvertently laying the foundation for one of the major prejudices of modern thinking: the presupposition that it was possible to have a point of view that was not a view from a particular point. He, and the modernist thinkers who followed him, believed that objectivity was possible and ideal. They believed that the kind of objectivity found in mathematics could be applied to our understanding of the world. The mathematical model was thought to provide the type of certainty that would overcome the vast variety of opinions and perspectives that plagued other areas of inquiry. Because it only accepted those things that were absolutely certain, the mathematical method was thought to put an end to any "prejudice in judgments."[5]

After establishing the principle of accepting only that which is certain, Descartes sets forth the second step in the method:

…divide up each of the difficulties…into as many parts as possible and as seemed requisite in order that it might be resolved in the best manner possible.[6]

For Descartes, breaking larger units into subunits is necessary if we want to avoid contradiction. Without analyzing things into ever-smaller units contradictions are inevitable. Consider for a moment the classic thought experiment about the identity of Socrates: Socrates is *and* is not a father. He is both the father of two particular sons *and* he is not the father of a particular dog.[7] In order to eliminate this contradiction, we need to think of his identity, not as a single identity that unites a great number of qualities and relations, but as something that can be broken down and analyzed into this particular aspect or that particular relationship. Under such analysis, Socrates is a father in one relationship but not a father in another relationship. In theory, all of the aspects of a particular thought(s) could be segregated until all contradictions and ambiguities disappear.

Another reason to analytically divide things into ever smaller parts is to increase control over the physical world. For Descartes, knowledge was for the purpose of mastery over nature. Descartes claimed that human life was less than ideal because of our lack of sufficient knowledge. If we had sufficient knowledge, we could overcome many of life's woes.

I am sure that there is no one, even among those who make its study a profession, who does not confess that all that men know is almost nothing in comparison with what remains to be known; and that we could be free of an infinitude of maladies both of body and mind, and even also possibly of the infirmities of age, if we had sufficient knowledge of their causes…[8]

We suffer from disease, aging, and ultimately death because we do not know enough to cure such problems. Knowledge could solve these problems, but unfortunately, says Descartes, our lives are too short and our minds too slow to accumulate the knowledge needed to find solutions to such problems. If our lives were extended for hundreds of years, or if the rate at which we learned was enormously accelerated, perhaps we could acquire the vast knowledge needed to solve our problems. Since we can neither extend our lives, nor the rate at which we learn,

Descartes suggested the idea of specialization, whereby we narrow our individual focus to master a particular area of learning.

Before Descartes and the modern period, individuals of the Renaissance typically committed themselves to a vast variety of interests and talents, ranging from painting and astronomy to literature and philosophy. Of course, such a variety of interests took an enormous amount of time out of one's life. It seemed that little time was left for research into specialized topics, such as cancer or aging. Descartes' suggestion is that, instead of being educated in all areas of learning, individuals should specialize in one area only. This approach would shorten an individual's education and allow more time for research in a narrow specialized area. If people were to devote fifty years of their lives to study a particular kind of cancer, they, or their students, or the students of their students would eventually come to know all there was to know about that cancer and thereby develop remedies. "By joining together the lives and labors of many, we should collectively proceed much further than any one in particular could succeed in doing."[9]

Interestingly, this partitioning of the world is not according to natural divisions but according to "the best manner possible." In the past, when analyzing the world into different kinds of things, divisions were made along what were considered natural lines or according to boundaries found in nature. The medieval Aristotelians thought that an active intellect gave us the ability to know the forms by which God had organized the world. Thus, many medieval thinkers claimed that they had a basis for dividing up the world according to natural or God-given boundaries. Descartes, however, was a believer in what became known as "the corpuscular philosophy," as were Locke, Newton, Galileo, Boyle, and a host of other seventeenth-century thinkers. The corpuscular philosophy, which would eventually evolve into atomic chemistry, had at its base the idea that what established natural kinds were not Aristotelian forms but microscopic, "corpuscular" structures. The essence of water, then, was not an Aristotelian form but something more like bonded molecules (what we now refer to as H_2O). Of course, in the seventeenth century, the precise exploration of this corpuscular or atomic level was not possible. Nevertheless, Descartes and his contemporaries believed that there was this deeper reality—even if it was inaccessible to them. Thus, without access to this deeper reality, but no longer believing in Aristotelian forms, Descartes' suggestion is to divide the world according to human purposes. What is most useful to our purpose, thought Descartes, is that we solve our problems of disease, aging, and death. The divisions we make, then, are not for the sake of replicating an order found in nature, which would be impossible given a belief in the corpuscular philosophy, but for the purpose of mastering the actual function of nature.

The ancients may have thought that they were following natural divisions in classifying and understanding whales as fish, bats as birds, and humans as land animals. However, if it better suits our purpose to classify the abovementioned animals as mammals, we should do so.

> [We are to] carry on [our] reflections in due order, commencing with objects that were the most simple and easy to understand, in order to rise little by little, or by degrees, to knowledge of the most complex, assuming an order, even if a fictitious one.[10]

This assumed, fictitious order is necessary since the actual order of nature is hidden on the corpuscular level. Accordingly, then, we must create an order for ourselves. For Descartes, and many of the modernist thinkers who followed, the organizing principle of life was to solve problems based on clear and distinct ideas like those of mathematics rather than relying on a correspondence to nature. If we cannot discover the God-established basis for the natural order that is hidden on the corpuscular level, a sense of reasoned certainty founded upon clear and distinct ideas must substitute as our criterion for truth.

The Cartesian equation of truth as a kind of scientific, mathematical certainty quickly spread and found its way into nearly all areas of inquiry during the seventeenth, eighteenth, and nineteenth centuries. This new quest for truth as the kind of certainty we find with clear and distinct ideas rather than a mirroring of nature, as it had been for many ancients and medievals, spread throughout the modern period. Theologians, no less than others, were influenced by the modernist way of thinking and they began to mold theories and doctrines accordingly. Of course, theologians did not go so far as to boast that their theories were founded upon *a priori* certainty (such as in mathematics). They did, however, produce ever narrower and more precise doctrines whose every part fit neatly together and resulted in a wonderfully comprehensive "order," even if a fictitious one.

Postmodern Versus Premodern

In spite of all we have been told about the intolerance of the medieval church, it did manage to hold together a cohesive body of believers amid a variety of theological ideology. Theologians such as John Duns Scotus (1270–1308) or William of Ockham (1288–1348), for example, did not develop new churches, nor were they excommunicated for their very different ideas. Instead, different ways of understanding faith were tolerated in ways that seemed impossible to later generations. By the time of the modern era, differences were no longer tolerated because our understand of the *truth* was now thought to be narrow and precise like the truths of mathematics.

One of the primary reasons for the premodern, flexible interpretation of truth is that for many centuries Christians argued that Scripture—the root of all truth—did not have a single, univocal meaning. They interpreted the quest for truth as a process of unfolding the infinite, sometimes hidden, meaning of sacred Scripture. Saint Augustine (354–430 CE), for example, would have thought that mathematics and the science of modernity, with their certain and precise meanings, were poor models for understanding the truth of Scripture. Speaking of the creation account in the Book of Genesis, Augustine says:

> Although I hear people say "Moses meant this" or "Moses meant that," I think it more truly religious to say "Why should he not have had both meanings in mind, if both are true? And if others see in the same words a third, or a fourth, or any number of true meanings, why should we not believe that Moses saw them all? There is only one God, who caused Moses to write the Holy Scripture in the way best suited to the minds of great numbers of men who would all see truths in them, though not the same truths in each case."
>
> For my part I declare resolutely and with all my heart that if I were called upon to write a book which was to be vested with the highest authority, I should prefer to write it in such a way that a reader could find re-echoed in my words whatever truths he was able to apprehend. I would rather write in this way than impose a single true meaning so explicitly that it would exclude all others.[11]

The theology of postmodern Christianity resonates with Augustine. Because the postmodern Christian understands that language is not like mathematics, whose elements have fixed and universal meanings, one cannot be certain that contemporary interpretations of Scripture are consistent with the intention of the ancient writer(s). Augustine says, for example, "How do you know that Moses meant his word to be taken in the way that you explain them?"[12] To those who claim that they alone know an exact and precise meaning of Scripture, Augustine comments:

> [They do so] not because they are men of God or because they have seen in the heart of Moses, your servant, that their expla-nation is the right one, but simply because they are proud. They have no knowledge of the thoughts in his mind, but they are in love with their own opinions, not because they are true, but because they are their own.[13]

According to Augustine, pride and ownership are at the base of such claims to truth. This is also the view of the postmodern Christian who sees modernity's quest for absolute, certain knowledge according to the Cartesian, mathematical model as motivated by pride and a de-sire for mastery. Speaking against modernity's view of certain knowl-edge, Merold Westphal, a contemporary philosopher from Fordham University, says something very reminiscent of Augustine:

> The longing for Absolute knowledge, which presents itself as the love of Truth, is less a desire to submit one's thought to the way things are than a desire to compel the world to submit to our conceptual mastery.[14]

Like Augustine, the postmodern Christian sees the modern desire for the truth as a desire to possess. A truth that is narrow, precise, and certain is much more easily possessed than one that is broad, multifari-ous, and uncertain.

A Postmodern Understanding

Today, the modern notion of a univocal truth based on certainty after the mathematical model is difficult to defend. We now know that the method that Descartes thought was going to remove all prejudices was itself a prejudice. There is no escape from our prejudices. We all have perspectival filters through which we experience the world. These filters provide a variety of different lights by which the truth is illumined. This is at least one of the reasons why *we see in a mirror, dimly* (1 Corinthians 13:12). That is, we see through the light of our own, limited, human perspectives, which produce a diversity of opinions concerning the truth. Modernity tried to remove these perspectival filters by only accepting as true those ideas that were either *a priori* or empirically certain. But the great mistake of modernity was to think that such a restriction would bring us closer to the truth rather than further from it. "We kid ourselves if we think we would get closer to the way things 'really' are if we could strip away our moods and our practices in order to become pure reason."[15]

Quite the opposite is the case. The reality is that the truth, insofar as human beings have access to it, is *always* perspectival. For us to desire a certain, objective reality is to wish to have access to the truth as God alone has access to it.

> To know things in themselves, things as they really are, would be to know them as God would know them. But since all the categories of human understanding are schematized in terms of time and since God sees everything under the aspect of eternity, there is a great gulf fixed between human and divine understanding, with the result that we can know things as they appear to us, but not as they are in themselves.[16]

Many consider such a limited understanding of the truth as less than ideal. Indeed, many reject such a perspectival view of the truth. They claim that since there is no way to measure which perspective is correct and which wrong, all views of the truth become equally viable and a wild relativism is the result. Jesus, on the other hand, tells us that there is a criterion for truth, but it is much more subjective than many want to accept. That is, he says that we can judge a thing by its fruit. *"The good person out of the good treasure of the heart produces good, and the evil person out of evil treasure produces evil; for it is out of the abundance of the heart that the mouth speaks"* (Luke 6:45).

In other words, what we bring to our experience is what produces the kind of fruit that bears good (or evil) results, and we can judge our perspectives by this fruit. Contemporary science operates on this same pragmatic principle. Today, scientific perspectives, hypotheses, and theories are driven by results. The many advances of technology stand as evidence for the "truth" of those perspectives and theories. For the Christian, however, the ultimate fruit by which we judge our perspectives is how fully those perspectives allow us to come into the life that the gospel promises.

Many of us seek more and more objectivity so that we can judge the correctness of one perspective over another. But there is no such objective criterion apart from the fruit of our individual, subjective perspectives. This causes many to cling to the kind of objective certainty modernity purported to offer.

Others who realize that this myth of modernity is no longer a viable option sometimes interpret the lack of objective standards as the result of our sinfulness—that is, we are limited due to the Fall. There is a long tradition among Christians who have believed that our fallenness has somehow affected our knowledge. There may be some merit to this idea, but it might not be in the way that most think. It may not be that the Fall caused us to lose the kind of ideal knowledge of which Descartes dreamt. Rather, instead of preventing us from achieving the Cartesian ideal of knowledge, sin may actually be what has caused us to think that such a notion of knowledge is ideal. That is, it is not that the Fall destroyed our ability to know, but rather that it perverted the way we want to know. Our sin is that we desire to know as God knows rather than to know as is proper for human beings. What is proper for human beings is to know through a sense of awe, wonder, and mystery. Biblical knowing is personal rather than objective, but human beings have a tendency to want to know the world as object. That desire reached a pinnacle with the modern period.

To the contrary, the Christian ideal is to know a God who is a person, and our knowledge of any person involves the mystery of trying to grasp the intentional meaning they wish to communicate. For example, my wife is a mystery to me. She is not, however, an unknowable mystery but she is infinitely knowable. Indeed, the more time I spend with her, the better sense I get of what is in her head and heart. Likewise, the more I read Derrida, the more I get an idea of what is in his head and heart. My understanding of both my wife and Derrida does not bring me any closer to an understanding of what is true concerning an objective reality but what is true concerning a person and their perspective concerning the world. Of course, this is what we as Christians should be seeking as well. It is not an objective reality that I am after, but the personal understanding Jesus has of that reality.

All this is not to say that modernity was completely devoid of merit. It did lay the foundations for a technology that "works." But the great evil of modernity was to discredit any subjective or personal knowing by insisting that all knowing be objective, certain, and devoid of mystery. The goal of modernity was to reduce everything to that which could be understood in the way that mathematics is understood—with certainty and precision rather than wonder and awe. This is the real suppression of the truth of which the Scripture speaks (see Romans 1:18). It is a suppression of the fact that our thoughts are not God's thoughts (see Isaiah 55:8).

The science of today has corrected many of these excesses of modernity, but at least some of the credit for those corrections has to be given to the postmodern critics of modernity who have been around since the time of David Hume (1711–1776). The error exposed by these critics of modernity is the Cartesian notion that ideas that appear to us to be clear and distinct are certain and therefore can be either seen as God's truth or a substitute for God's truth. A healthy, postmodern suspicion concerning the nature and extent of our access to such truth is the remedy for such an error.

There is, however, a more sinister element involved in modernity's notion of truth. That more sinister element is the fact that, having once established the foundations for knowledge in *a priori* or empirical certainty, it was then easy to take the next step. If only that which could be known through *a priori* or empirical certainty was true, why believe that things that cannot be accessed in such ways exist at all? Thus, the modern world became truncated and reduced to only that which could be known through the approved method of modern science.

A hundred years ago, William James (1842–1910) criticized such a view and claimed that it was irrational to maintain that something, which possibly could exist, did not exist simply because it was not knowable by a particular rational or empirical criterion.[17] As irrational as it might sound, however, this had become the dominant view, and it left us with a very small world, devoid of any spiritual or transcendent reality.

Today, we know that the truth of our reality is something much more than what the modern thinkers had led us to imagine. We now know that we do not get to reality through a reduction down to a bedrock of certainty. The reality of the human condition is reached by addition rather than reduction. It is composed of both what is given to us in our experience and the perspective that we bring to that experience. For example, a person with schizophrenia brings something different to his or her experience and thereby lives in a different reality than the rest of us. We all bring something to what constitutes our reality. This is as true of the Christian as anyone else. Reality for the Christian is not found in what is objectively given to us in experience, but is largely a matter of what we bring to our experience. It is our perspectival understanding that molds and shapes our reality, just as the schizophrenic person's reality is shaped by what he or she brings to the experience. The tendency of the modernists may have been to focus on the givenness of our experience in order to change it. What is most important, however, is that we change our perspective so that we might better understand the circumstances in which we find ourselves. We should desire not a solution or way to escape from our circumstances, but rather a better perspective or understanding of those circumstances so that we would know the fullness of life God has for us.

Søren Kierkegaard (1813–1855) had spoken of the truth of Christianity as being subjective rather than objective. One way to understand subjectivity is to realize that the truth of Christianity is not defined by what is outside us but rather by what is within us. Reality is largely about perspective, or the mindset and heart's attitude that we bring to the external circumstances of our lives. The correct perspective is the one that allows us to come more fully into the image and likeness of Jesus.

Although true for Christians of all ages, one of the great insights of postmodernism is that reality is perspectival. Ultimate reality for the Christian should never have been the kind of objective reality that the sciences of modernity sought. Christian reality requires that we bring something to our experience, and something more than mental hardware. In order for us to come into the fullness of life that God has for us, we must bring faith to our experience and believe that God intends a blessing, even in the worst of circumstances.

The fullness of the Christian reality is not achieved by eliminating all prejudice, as was the ambition of modernity. In order to dwell in the phenomenal reality God has for us, we need to bring gratitude to every experience and believe that God can use any circumstance to the ultimate good of transforming us into the likeness of his Son. Therefore, unlike modernity, which attempted to eliminate all prejudice, faith requires a prejudice. It requires the prejudice of seeing a blessing in circumstances that appear to others to be evil. For the Christian, our ultimate reality—our heaven or hell—ultimately rests in the prejudicial perspective we bring to the givenness of our experience and not the givenness itself.

Jesus came looking for faith on the earth, and he finds it, not in the people with the correct religious practices or theological doctrines, but in people with a certain prejudice that caused them to see God at work in circumstances that others perceived as evil. For example, Jesus tells a story of how one bypasser (a supposedly religious man) sees a man beaten and left for dead as one accursed by God and therefore evil, but another bypasser (a Samaritan) sees in that same circumstance an opportunity to manifest God's mercy (see Luke 10:30–37). The Canaanite woman, whom Jesus compares to a dog, saw that God's mercy extends even to the dogs, and Jesus praised her faith (see Matthew 15:21–28). Such people are the very antithesis of the enlightened thinkers who shaped modernity. The modernists sought to reduce human experience to free it of its prejudices. People of faith, however, bring their prejudicial faith to every experience.

Furthermore, whereas Descartes' project was to establish a basis for trust in human knowledge, people of faith, like those of postmodernity, are suspicious of human knowledge. That suspicion, however, has brought them closer to understanding the truth of the human condition. They may not be able to make a claim to certainty as did their Enlightenment predecessors, but they do possess a view of the world that is more genuinely human. Such a postmodern view seems much more compatible with faith and much more conducive to producing saints.

[S]aints will be wiser but less cocksure, happier but less self-satisfied, humbler in acknowledging his ignorance yet better equipped to understand the relationship of words to things, of systematic reasoning to the unfathomable Mystery which it tries, forever vainly, to comprehend.[18]

Certainly our concept of truth lies at the base of our understanding and thus shapes our Christian life. Having considered both the modern and postmodern notions of that concept, it would seem that the postmodern notion is both more conducive to gospel living and more realistic concerning the human condition. With that concept established, we now move on to other concepts essential to the Christian life. The first of these is faith.

Questions for Reflection

1. Define religious truth.
2. What is the difference between objective and subjective truth?
3. What role should science and mathematics play in the search for religious truth?
4. How much access to truth is available to human beings?

2

Faith as Journey

In the last chapter, faith appeared to be some sort of prejudice that we bring to our experience, but here we will learn that faith can take many forms. Perhaps faith is broader than what we had been led to imagine by our modern culture. When we read that it is impossible to please God without faith (see Hebrews 11:6), we naturally want to know the exact meaning of faith so that we might be pleasing to God. Unfortunately, as explored previously, our interpretation of life has been greatly influenced by a culture whose ideals for knowledge were modeled according to the kind of precise reasoning we find in mathematics. Consequently, most of us have a concept of faith that is more the product of a modern scientific culture than the gospels. In light of this fact, we should treat our concept of faith with a certain suspicion. By doing so, we are able to receive Scripture—to accept the voice of the Spirit—in ways that are otherwise impossible when we limit ourselves to imagining that we have a correct concept of faith. Our suspicion, I believe, allows us to unlock a more gospel-based concept of faith that remains hidden without such suspicion.

In recent years I have realized many of my own prejudicial errors. For example, some time ago, I published a paper about the dynamics of faith.[1] I intended to show that there was merit on both sides of the long-standing debate over whether faith was emotive, as many had claimed, or if it was something like a propositional belief supported by reason, as maintained by many others. My argument was that faith initially begins in the emotive realm as hope, but then, as God demonstrates his faithfulness toward us, our faith is validated by our experience and thus supportable through reason. *Faith is the assurance of things hoped for* (Hebrews 11:1). We begin with hope, but over time we gather evidence to substantiate our hope. In other words, as we look to God in hope, and he continually meets us in our need, we have something more than hope in his faithfulness, and our faith becomes a belief that is supported by reason.

For support, I turned to Mark's Gospel, where we see faith covering a spectrum that extends from the emotive realm of hope (perhaps a mixture of belief and doubt) to the more experienced, cognitive realm (where beliefs are supported by reason). For example, Mark tells us that a man approached Jesus and asked him to cast out an evil spirit from his son.

> "...if you are able to do anything, have pity on us and help us."
> Jesus said to him, "If you are able!—All things can be done for
> the one who believes." Immediately the father of the child cried
> out, "I believe; help my unbelief!" (Mark 9:22–24).

It would seem that the simple belief (or faith) of this man was largely rooted in a desire (or hope) rather than any reasoned confidence in Jesus' proposition that *all things can be done for the one who believes.* We have no indication that the man was a follower of Jesus or even knew much about him. As the story proceeds, we learn that this man's hope— even if accompanied by a certain amount of doubt—was enough to cast the demon from his son. By contrast, however, the disciples' faith in this same situation was rooted more in experience and reason than in hope. The fate of the disciples' sons was not at stake, so their hope most likely was not at the fatherly level. But they certainly would have had a "faith" that was more reason-based than the faith of the boy's father. After all, unlike the father of the child, the disciples had experienced multiple instances of Jesus' ability and willingness to heal and work miracles. Thus, their faith was much more a matter of having good reason to believe in Jesus' ability to heal. The faith of the boy's father, on the other hand, was much less a matter of reason and more a matter of hope. It would seem that the disciples' faith is a more mature faith in that it has the support of reason in addition to whatever hope lay at its root.

When two people marry, they may trust or have faith in each other, but without the benefit of years of experience, their faith is typically fueled by hope. In time, that faith may become more than hope as they give each other reason to have faith. The same seems to be the case in regard to our faith in God. Thus, according to my original article about the dynamics of faith, we begin in the emotive realm of hope but move toward a more reason-based faith over time as we experience God's grace.

My philosophy students challenged my view and forced me to re-think my theory. One student, in particular, cited the same example of Mark 9:22–24 but added the additional character of the boy's mother. If we imagine that the mother was not at the site of the miracle and knew nothing of Jesus until her son returned home healed, we have an example of someone who comes to faith in Jesus through reasonable evidence from the very beginning. In the case of the boy's mother, faith does not progress from hope to reason. Thus, it would appear that faith can also be initiated by reason.

Although faith does not always proceed from the emotive to the rational, I continue to believe that faith development contains both elements. If the boy's mother enters into a faith relationship with God, there will be future instances where her faith will rest more on the passion of hope than on reasonable evidence. Furthermore, although faith does not always need to proceed from the emotive toward the rational, that does seem to be the general pattern, although it is certainly not the only pattern.

Faith as Relational Journey

Faith begins with us becoming aware of God either through blind hope or reasoned assurance, but proceeds by God producing faith in us through what might best be described as a journey. If the Christian life is a life of faith, then perhaps all points throughout the span of our lives may be parts of that faith journey, and consequently faith may take many forms. Ultimately, however, the end of this faith journey is something that God produces and not something we muster through passion or reason.

Martin Luther (1483–1546) was correct by claiming that, ultimately, the core of Christian life is grounded in faith and not works. Of course,

31

throughout most of our life, faith is a work that we initiate, either through our own passion or some type of reasoning based in theology or even through miraculous experiences. We say that such things are not works because some mysterious faith has been given to us and that faith is what lies at the bottom of our passion or reasoning. In other words, "works" are the product of our faith—the fruit of our inspired belief system. The gift of faith, however, is not merely the point from which we begin our journey, but it is also the end toward which we are being drawn. Furthermore, the ultimate faith toward which we are being led in this journey is something that God and God alone provides. We may struggle or "work" to accept God's gift, but it is God who is orchestrating the journey. Consider the example of the apostle Peter.

> "Simon, Simon, listen! Satan has demanded to sift all of you like wheat, but I have prayed for you that your own faith may not fail; and you, when once you have turned back, strengthen your brothers" (Luke 22:31–32).

In this passage, Luke compares the impact of Satan on the faith of Peter (whose faith is strengthened by Jesus' prayer) with the impact of Satan on the faith of Judas (the one who fell; see Acts 1:15–19). The Greek for "all of you" is plural and the implication is that Satan's sifting applies to all people. Here the prayers of Jesus protect Peter—and thus the entire Church—from the fate of Judas. The second verse shifts to the singular—that is, to Peter—and we discover that he is in need, or will be in need, of "conversion" or "turning back." The reference has less to do with Peter's acceptance of Christ—after all, he already proclaimed Jesus as "the Messiah, the Son of the living God" (Matthew 16:16)—than it does with his moral strength for his journey toward God. That is, Peter's "turning back" is founded on the Greek epistrepsas, meaning "moral conversion" (see also Luke 17:14, and Acts 3:19, 9:35, 11:21, 14:15, 15:19, 26:18, 20). The prayer of Jesus will eventually lead Peter to a new understanding of himself (particularly his weakness) so that he can understand God more fully. Ultimately, Luke's theology assures the Church that the Lord can save us all from the power of Satan, again and again, just as he saved Peter.

We can assume that Jesus' prayer accomplished its purpose, and that Peter's faith did not utterly fail. But if Peter's faith was not squelched, then his denial of Jesus shortly before the crucifixion must have been part of his faith and thus part of his journey into an ever-greater knowledge of God. Luke is known for contrasting the obedient journey of Jesus alongside the turbulent, misguided faith journey of the disciples to demonstrate the process of conversion or change that all must experience in a life of faith. Here, Peter becomes a model for lifelong conversion.

It seems evident that as of Luke 22:31–32 Peter did not fully know Jesus despite being on the Mount of Transfiguration or having walked on water at Jesus' command. Equally, Peter apparently did not know who he was before he denied Jesus, and real conversion requires that we come to see who God really is and who we really are. Conversion does not seem to be achieved without death and resurrection. For Peter, it begins on the night that Jesus was arrested. After professing that he was willing to die with Jesus, three times Peter denies ever having known him. The faith that took three years and unbelievable miracles to build was completely set aside in one dark night. So much for Peter's more usual passion, perseverance, and all the testimony of miracles that he had witnessed. In that dark night, he fell despite his passionate claim to faith and all the miracles he had witnessed. But it seems that Peter's dark night was necessary to bring him to the ultimate faith that God wished to give him. In order to have a faith based on knowledge of the true God, Peter first had to see who he truly was, and that seems to come about only through stages of death and resurrection, of dying (denying) and rising (converting or turning) toward God.

Death and Resurrection

At its base, Christianity is always about death and resurrection. Something must die to bring forth new life. In order for us to come into a resurrected life, there must first be the death of who we think we are. To see who we truly are, the illusion of who we *think* we are must be destroyed. Peter thinks he knows who he is. He is a devout follower of Jesus for whom he is willing to die if necessary. But in that dark night, Peter discovers that despite his best intentions he was not able to sustain his faith. But as Peter experiences the death of his own faith, and the death of who he thought he was, he is about to see who God truly is.

33

The revelation of who God truly is comes when Peter encounters the risen Christ. But it is not merely the fact that Peter has witnessed Jesus raised from the dead that reveals God to him. God reveals his nature through the risen Christ who never mentions Peter's lapse in faith but instead gives him three chances to say "I love you" (see John 21:15–17). Unlike you or I, who would certainly have had something to say to a friend who had failed so miserably in their faithfulness, Jesus never mentions it. At that point, Peter sees who God really is, and that nothing can separate him from the love of God, not even his own lack of faith. Prior to that point, Peter might have known some things about the nature of God. He may have even known that Jesus was the Son of God, but it was not until his own personal encounter with the risen Christ that he knew the true nature of God and that nothing could separate him from God's love. This is the ultimate point of faith toward which we are all being drawn, but we only seem to reach it through that dark night of the soul when our own faith is shaken at its core. It is only when our own faith fails that we receive a faith that is truly from God. That is the death that is at the base of the resurrected life.

Of course, Jesus is the ultimate manifestation of faith through death and resurrection. In the gospels, Jesus works miracles, heals the lame, and raises the dead. He does these things faithfully as the beloved Son of God, but the end of his faith journey leads him into rejection, suffering, death, and resurrection. He models the dynamic of all faith journeys. Along with the miracles and the glorious revelations come rejection, suffering, death, and resurrection.

The gospel shows us how everyone is to come to the ultimate faith God has for us. Like Jesus, we are to have a faith that is based in our hope in God and our having seen God meet us time and time again, but such faith never terminates in a complete understanding of God. We are always on the road. We constantly search for certitude that nothing can separate us from God's love. When we are rejected and suffer, it is quite natural that we experience a loss of faith and the sense that we are being abandoned by God. Jesus manifests this most important aspect of the faith journey when he cries, *"My God, my God, why have you forsaken me?"* (Matthew 27:46 and Mark 15:34). Some argue that Jesus is merely quoting Psalm 22—which, no doubt he is—but we must remember that he is fully divine *and* fully human and, as such, his cry reveals everyone's faith experience. Ultimately, in our faith journey, we are brought to a place of death in our soul—a place where we feel abandoned by God. It is a place where we are able to muster very little in the form of faith and all seems lost. When we come out of that death experience alive, we have a new faith and a new understanding of God. We realize that it was not the greatness of our faith that brought us through, but the greatness of God.

I once heard someone say that no one was more surprised on Easter Sunday morning than Jesus. To many that may seem blasphemous, and I thought the same thing when I first heard it. Jesus knew what was going to happen to him. He had prophesied what was going to happen, so it could not have been a surprise. Of course, it was a surprise in the way that we are all surprised by what seems to be a lack of faith when we enter the dark night of the soul. We may boldly speak of the promises that God has made to us and hold those promises in what we call faith, but when circumstances turn against us and we do not feel God's presence in those circumstances, his promises seem very far from us. This is what everyone who walks in faith eventually experiences. Of course, it's common today to reject the humanness of Jesus. Many people want Jesus to be purely God. They much prefer a divine Jesus to a human one because it's easier to worship Jesus as God than follow him as our example of how to be human. But God became a man to show us how to be human. Ultimately, Jesus defines our human journey of faith with respect to God's relationship with us. To be human is to know that we are a beloved daughter or son of God and that nothing can separate us from our Father's love, and the only way we come to that ultimate faith relationship is through death and resurrection.

Certainly Jesus had faith when he was raising the dead and walking on water, but his faith on Easter Sunday morning was a different kind of faith. It was the kind of faith that only comes through death and resurrection, and God wishes us all to come to that ultimate place of faith. We, however, resist and attempt to find another way. The other way so many of us choose is to make Jesus wholly God so that we can merely worship him rather than follow him. In truth, however, Jesus is both divine *and* human, and we are to both worship him and follow him, but, if we have trouble doing both, his preference seems to be that we follow him rather than worship him.

Jesus never tells us to worship him. Only twice is the phrase "worship me" used in the gospels. Once is when Satan asks Jesus to worship him (see Matthew 4:9, also Luke 4:7). The other appearance of the phrase "worship me" occurs when Jesus quotes the prophet Isaiah.

"Isaiah prophesied rightly about you [hypocrites] when he said: / 'This people honors me with their lips, / but their hearts are far from me; / in vain do they worship me, / teaching human precepts as doctrines'" (Matthew 15:7–9, also Mark 7:6–7).

By contrast, Jesus insistently tells us to follow him. He uses the phrase "follow me" seventeen times, and in three of those instances he very specifically tells us to take up our cross and follow him (see Matthew 16:24 and Mark 8:34, 10:21). Of course, we would rather worship Jesus than follow him, because to follow him leads to rejection, suffering, and death. As much as we wish to deny it, that is where the Christian life of faith leads us. In order to come to truly know God, we must come to the end of ourselves—to the limits of our faith. That is where Jesus was led, and it is also where Peter and every other follower of Jesus are led. This is the way of faith that Jesus so beautifully models. It begins, where Jesus begins, with the awareness that he was the beloved son of God. Out of this faith that he is God's beloved, Jesus receives power from on high and works many miracles. There is, however, more to Jesus' faith experience and there is more to the faith experience of anyone else who wishes to become aware of the fact that they are God's beloved daughter or son. The ultimate faith experience that Jesus reveals is not found in the miracles he performs or the confidence he has in his Father's love. Rather it is found in the fact that he ultimately suffers rejection and death, but then returns to life.

Throughout most of our lives, faith is something that we muster through passion or reason, but the ultimate work of faith is something God does, not through some magical infusion but through a death and resurrection experience. During this time, we experience the death of all that had given meaning to our lives. Everything that we had believed and put such faith in seems lost. This painful experience precedes resurrection, and upon coming out of this death experience alive, we know God in a way that could only be revealed through death and resurrection. It is only through death and resurrection that we come to know that it was not by our faith that we had come into eternal life but by the sovereign hand of God. It is only through death and resurrection that we know that nothing can separate us from the love of God—not even our own lack of faith (see Romans 8:35–39).

We need to understand the meaning of death and resurrection so that when we are led into that place where our passion and theology fail and our faith has no support, we do not run from that holy place God has prepared for us. We need to remain under God's sovereign hand despite our desire to return to those early stages of faith where our confidence in God was so secure. We want that confidence and assurance we once had, and we see the death experience as something to be avoided at all cost. But *"unless a grain of wheat falls into the earth and dies, it remains just a single grain"* (John 12:24). Without death and resurrection, we never realize the full unity and communion God intends for us.

A Postmodern, Authentic Faith

The Christian life is one in which we are to dwell in God's presence, heal the sick, and work miracles; but that is only a portion of the gospel. Our ministry—that is, our personal context for living the gospel message— can have the negative effect of producing the illusion that there is something wonderful about *our* faith, or even that it is our faith that is the cause of God's love for us. It is only through death and resurrection that we come to know that our faith is very weak and not able to sustain us. But there is a faith that can raise the dead and it is God's alone.

We are brought to real conversion and given true faith, not through a ritual or confession of what we believe, but by coming to see God in all things, including suffering and death. The life of faith may begin when we become aware of God's blessings in our own lives, but its end is our becoming aware of God's presence through all phases of our lives. Since reality is conceptual, we will only be able to realize the fullness of God's kingdom when we have eyes to see and ears to hear God at work in all things, including our suffering and death experiences.

Some people live in hell on earth. They do not see God in anything. Most of us live somewhere between heaven and hell. We see God in this circumstance but not that circumstance, we see God in this person but not that person, in life but not death. The place to which God wants to bring us, however, is a place where we see God at work in all things, and we only come to that place through death and resurrection.

We need to have an expanded concept of faith. In the past, we have used different experiences of our faith journey to separate ourselves from one another. The people who were experiencing the emotive aspect of faith separated themselves from those who were having a more rational experience, and they all separated themselves from those who appeared to have lost their faith. Thankfully, God does not separate himself from us for such reasons. God knows that faith is a relationship which, over the course of time, takes many forms, and the only thing that is essential is that we stay in the relationship and allow God to bring us to an ever-greater understanding of who we are and who he is.

This concept of faith is very different from the idea of faith as merely a set of religious beliefs. It is a concept much broader than what we have come to expect because of the prejudices that we have inherited from the modern mindset. The modern mind was formed out of increasingly narrow and precise concepts, but, as we saw with the concept of faith, what we really need are broader concepts. This is not only true of faith but of other concepts as well. It is perhaps most especially true with our concept of love, which we turn to now.

Questions for Reflection

1. Can faith change over time?
2. How can a crisis affect faith?
3. Does God treat people differently based on their level of faith? Explain.
4. What are the most important things one can learn about God as faith increases?

3

The Concept of Love

Our concept of love, like our concept of faith, also seems to suffer from narrowness. This narrowness may be the result of a natural tendency that seeks to simplify our understanding, but it also has been fueled by modernity's prejudice for narrow and precise concepts such as in mathematics. As a result, our human concept of love seems very different from the concept of love that is attributed to God in Scripture. There are three primary differences between God's concept of love and the typical human concept of love: (1) love for the unlovely, (2) creation rather than acquisition, and (3) never-ending attention.

Loving the "Good and Beautiful"

Unlike human beings—who, for the most part, can only love and have affection for that which is good or beautiful—God, by contrast, has the capacity to love the unlovely, or at least what appears to be unlovely to us. That is, unlike human beings who seek a beloved who is at least as good or beautiful as they, God has chosen as the objects of his affection creatures who appear very inferior in goodness and beauty. Thus, God loves what seems unlovely. Of course, what we see is always a phenomenal reality—reality as it appears to us. In that apparent reality, we are indeed sinners who have pursued other gods and reaped the destruction that comes from that. In our flesh, which we tend to create for ourselves by identifying with the gods of this world (wealth, power, prestige), we are something very different from what God intended us to be. God, however, does not see us simply as that flesh that we project to the world. From God's perspective, we are his creation at the core of our being—his beloved daughters and sons. Furthermore, God fashioned us so that his creation would continue within us so that we would be made evermore into his likeness. God's desire is like a righteous father who loves his children and wants them to follow in his ways. This desire requires that we would be changed and made like him in our ability to love human beings, not because they are good or beautiful, but because they are God's creation.

Reality is certainly perspectival, and we have considerable liberty in establishing our perspective. We can choose a human perspective that views others as good or bad—deserving of love or undeserving of love. Or, we can choose a divine perspective and see other human beings as God's beloved daughters and sons—and therefore our sisters and brothers.

By seeing God as a loving father, we also see that our idea of sin, as will be explained in the next chapter, is not an offense to God's honor. Rather, our sin causes God to suffer because it is what keeps his beloved children from the fullness of life that he desires for them. The idea of a suffering God is difficult for many to accept, just as it was difficult for the religious people of Jesus' day to accept the idea of a suffering Messiah. Such difficulties are the result of our thinking that God's love is like our own. We cannot love our enemies because we see nothing good or beautiful in them. God loves his enemies because they are first and foremost his creation, and we are to love our enemies because they are first and foremost our sisters and brothers.

Unfortunately, such a notion of God as the Father of a species of prodigals goes very much against who we imagine God to be. We imagine that God is like us because we believe that we have a correct concept of love. Being content with our human concept of love makes it quite natural for us to anthropomorphize God and imagine that God, who is most good and most beautiful, must only love that which is good and beautiful like himself. Since he is perfect, he must only love perfect things. This very human concept of God is what we find in Aristotle. Aristotle had imagined that God must be involved with that which is most good.

He therefore thought that God must be involved in contemplation, which Aristotle (a philosopher) believed was the greatest good. Furthermore, the object of God's contemplation must be focused on God himself, since God is that which is most good and most beautiful.[1] "Therefore it must be of itself that the divine thought thinks (since it is the most excellent of things)."[2]

This, however, is the nature of human rather than divine love, and it is not what we find in the gospels. It is we, and not God, who focus our attention on that which we believe to be most excellent. It is we who only love that which we deem to be good or beautiful, and we cease to love when the objects of our affection are discovered to be less than what we consider perfect. This is the nature of human beings. It is our affection that is limited, and we are the ones who love only perfect things. When we imagine that something is no longer good or beautiful, our love for it ends. We marry spouses because we believe them to be good or beautiful, but when we discover their imperfections, our love fades. Some of us even leave them in order to find objects of affection that are more perfect in goodness or beauty. We divorce our spouses and disown our children because of their lack of perfection. This is the nature of human love, which only loves that which is good or beautiful.

In one regard, it is good that our human love seeks the beautiful, for such desire causes us to seek God. Nevertheless, although the desire for the good and the beautiful may initiate us into a relationship with God, it is not what God ultimately has for us. The divine love into which God is calling us is about learning to see beauty in all of creation. The Christian life is ultimately about transformation, but it is not simply about being transformed into creatures who are morally good and meet some imagined standard that makes us proper objects of God's love. Rather, Christian life involves the more radical process of being made into God's likeness and taking on the unique nature of his love. The point of the Christian life, in whatever form it takes, is for us to be transformed and made evermore into his divine likeness. In taking on the nature of his love, we must become lovers, not of who (or what) we deem good or beautiful, but lovers of God's creation. The good news of the gospel is that God loves us in spite of our sin, and that God wants us to become like him so that we can love others in spite of their sin. They may be sinners, but they are first and foremost God's beloved sons and daughters, and therefore they are also our brothers and sisters.

One of the reasons we have trouble seeing the sinner as the object of love is because we think that their sin has separated them from God's love, and therefore they should be separated from our love as well. There is some truth to the idea that their sin has separated them from God, but it is not that sin causes God to withdraw his love. Rather, sin is our turning away from God. The good news is that our separation from God can be overcome simply by returning to him, since he is the father who awaits the return of the prodigal with open arms. The message of the gospel is that forgiveness and restoration are freely given, and God is more accessible than we had previously thought. In fact, the gospel begins with John baptizing people for the forgiveness of sin with water from the Jordan River. Unlike the rituals that had to be performed in order to forgive sin and overcome separation from God in the Old Testament, the forgiveness of sin, as presented in the gospel, is now as accessible and abundant as the water of the Jordan River. Jesus tells us that the kingdom of God has been opened to everyone, and we are not held back from God's great banquet because he has deemed us unworthy, but rather that we do not enter because we have deemed God unworthy.

> *"Someone gave a great dinner and invited many. At the time for the dinner he sent his slave to say to those who had been invited, 'Come; for everything is ready now.' But they all alike began to make excuses. The first said to him, 'I have bought a piece of land, and I must go out and see it; please accept my regrets.' Another said, 'I have bought five yoke of oxen, and I am going to try them out; please accept my regrets.' Another said, 'I have just been married, and therefore I cannot come.' So the slave returned and reported this to his master. Then the owner of the house became angry and said to his slave, 'Go out at once into the streets and lanes of the town and bring in the poor, the crippled, the blind, and the lame'"* (Luke 14:16–21).

With this parable nothing is required to come to the banquet God has prepared for us, and our separation from God is totally on our part and not God's. In the version of this story that appears in the Gospel of Matthew a garment is required, just as so many parables speak of requirements that must be met in order to follow in the way that Jesus has prepared. But our not being at the banquet that God has prepared for us is a result of our choice to be somewhere else and not a result of God thinking that we are not worthy.

It is also interesting to note that what we choose over being in God's presence is not usually criminal, such as a crack house or bordello. More than likely, we choose to do things that we think are good, like marrying a "beautiful" person or doing "good" business. Certainly these are not the kinds of things for which God would condemn us? According to the parable, we are not excluded from the banquet at all, but rather we exclude ourselves—not by committing immoral acts but by seeking our happiness in things apart from God. The good news is that the kingdom of God is open to everyone who would come. God's love is not restricted by narrow ideas of what is good or beautiful the way our human love is. The unworthy sinner is as much the object of God's love as the saint.

Transformation

As good as this news is, however, it is not the entire story. God's desire is that we would not only become the recipient of divine love, but that we would be transformed by it and made righteous as he is righteous. That righteousness, however, is not simply a matter of avoiding what our culture considers sin. It is rather a matter of taking on the divine virtue of being able to love God's unlovely children just as he does. This is the part of the Christian life that we find most distasteful and what we are least willing to embrace. We are all willing to follow Jesus into the power of his resurrection. We are even reluctantly willing to enter into the fellowship of his suffering. What we are often reluctant to do, however, is to follow him in his love for those who are not good—those who are, in fact, our enemies. This is the more difficult part of our transformation. In fact, it is so distasteful that we most often simply refuse to acknowledge this aspect of the gospel and instead insist that God's love is like our own, and God, like us, only loves his good and beautiful children. To do so, we must ignore the story of the prodigal son, or at least imagine that the older brother is somehow right in his refusal to rejoice in his brother's return and his father's forgiveness. Indeed, if we were really honest, most of us would have to admit that we identify with the older brother and resent the father's love and forgiveness for someone so underserving. Nearly all of us want to be rewarded for our goodness, and we want others to be punished when they do not measure up to our idea of goodness.

Our general experience with human beings is that we are loved more for good behavior and less for bad behavior. We come to expect the same from everyone, including God. The story of the prodigal tells us that God can love us no more than he already does, and his love for us does not increase or decrease because of our behavior. His is the love of a father for his daughters or sons, and the love of a creator toward his creation. Until we realize this, we remain like the older son who refuses to come to the banquet and celebrate the return of his brother.

Of course, the person in the story with whom we ought to ultimately identify is the father. The Christian life is a process of transformation, the end of which is to be made into God's likeness. That likeness amounts to becoming the father of the prodigal who loves, not because his sons are good or beautiful, but because they are his sons. Ultimately, we are to love others, not for their goodness or beauty, but because they are God's children and our brothers and sisters.

The reason it is so easy to ignore this story of the prodigal and imagine that God's love is like our own is because few of us have ever experienced anything like the kind of unconditional love that God has for us. Those who have experienced such love, either from God or one of his human agents, are able to enter into the transformative process whereby we too are made into creatures who, like Jesus, are able to love the unlovely. God desires such perfection for us—not that we would become morally pure and thus proper objects of divine affection, but that we would become like God and take on the capacity to love the unlovely.

Human Love as Acquisitive Love

The second important way that God's love differs from human love is found in the fact that human love is essentially acquisitive. We love those things that we can acquire to satisfy our many needs. God, on the other hand, is not needy and thus has no desire to acquire anything. This, however, does not mean that God is passionless or without desire. God certainly has desire, but his passion is not a desire to acquire but to create. This difference between human acquisitive love and God's love of creation is brought out in the story of Jonah. After Jonah had preached repentance to Nineveh, he sat down outside the city and waited to see what would become of it.

The LORD God appointed a bush, and made it come up over Jonah, to give shade over his head, to save him from his discomfort; so Jonah was very happy about the bush. But when dawn came up the next day, God appointed a worm that attacked the bush, so that it withered. When the sun rose, God prepared a sultry east wind, and the sun beat down on the head of Jonah so that he was faint and asked that he might die. He said, "It is better for me to die than to live."

But God said to Jonah, "Is it right for you to be angry about the bush?" And he said, "Yes, angry enough to die." Then the LORD said, "You are concerned about the bush, for which you did not labor and which you did not grow; it came into being in a night and perished in a night. And should I not be concerned about Nineveh, that great city, in which there are more than a hundred and twenty thousand people who do not know their right hand from their left, and also many animals?" (Jonah 4:6–11).

God says that Jonah was concerned for the bush for which he did not labor or make to grow. In fact, however, Jonah's only concern for the bush was that it brought him pleasure. That is the nature of human affection. We like those things that bring us pleasure or satisfy some need in us. Once the object of our affection no longer satisfies our need, our affection ceases. Jonah, in fact, did not care about the bush at all. His only concern was for his own need and what would satisfy that need.

God's love for Nineveh, however, is quite different. The people of Nineveh are his creation, and for that alone he loves them. His desire is to see his creation continue, and he knows that if the people of Nineveh could be brought to repentance and turn back toward him, there would be an ever-greater capacity for God to continue his creation within them. What this story communicates concerning God's love is that, unlike human love, which is basically a desire to have our needs gratified, God's love abounds with passion for his creation.

John Piper has written extensively on Jonathan Edwards' idea that the end for which God created the world is his glory. Of course, glory is another concept that we understand in an all-too-human way. Glory for us involves the increase of our wealth, power, or prestige to the ever-greater inflation of our egos. By contrast, God's glory, according to John

Piper and Jonathan Edwards, is his creation. God does everything for his creation or glory, but that glory involves the "ever-increasing joy of his people in that glory."[3] This glory is what motivates God just as our human, acquisitive love motivates us. It is what God loves to do—the thing for which he has a passion.

Thus, the question of whether God acts in his own interest or the interest of his beloved cannot be put to God the way it can be put to human beings. Since human love is acquisitive, when we acquire those things that satisfy our needs, we are satisfying our own desires and not the desires of others. Furthermore, the satisfying of our acquisitive desires often precludes others from satisfying their desires with the same object. If I love a woman and marry her to satisfy my desire, it precludes anyone else from satisfying their desires with her. By contrast, when God satisfies his desire and creates his glory within a beloved, it is as much in the beloved's interest as it is in God's, since the nature of his desire is to create the "ever-increasing joy of his people" by making them evermore into the likeness of his son.

> God in seeking his glory seeks the good of his creatures, because the emanation of his glory...implies the communicated excellency and happiness of his creatures. And in communicating his fullness for them, he does it for himself, because their good, which he seeks, is so much in union and communion with himself.[4]

Since God's love, which is so much a part of who he is, is a love of creation, it is no wonder that he is personified as *father*. Certainly, his love of creation is that of a father's love for his children. The other metaphor that Scripture uses to describe God's love—and is also descriptive of a creative love—is that of the intimacy between spouses. We especially see such language in Hosea, Revelation, the fifth chapter of Ephesians, and the Song of Solomon. Of course, there are many metaphorical aspects to such relationships, but sexual language is often used to describe the nature of God's love. The medieval Christian mystics, for example, often spoke of their encounters with God in sexual terms, and in her book *Passionate Spirituality*, Elizabeth Dreyer says, "It is precisely the experience of sexual love that gave rise to the language and metaphors of love used by the mystics in virtually every major religion."[5]

The sexual encounter between a husband and wife is surely marked by passion, as is the encounter between God and human beings. But more importantly, in both cases this passion leads to the creation of new life. Just as a husband impregnates a wife through passion, so too, God, out of his passion, impregnates those humans who are willing to become his bride. I would argue that this is a good way (perhaps the best way) to understand the seed parables of the New Testament. According to those parables, the seed is the word of God that serves as spiritual semen to produce new life within us.

God as Impregnator

In the seed parables, Jesus is the sower and we are the ones who receive his seed. In the Gospel of Luke, Jesus explains that *"the seed is the word of God"* (8:11). Some of the ground (some of humanity) is receptive to receiving the seed (the word) so that it might produce life. Although the analogy here is agricultural rather than biological, there does seem to be a strong parallel between this parable and the kind of sexual intimacy that is the subject of the Song of Solomon. Dreyer quotes Bernard of Clairvaux in his sermon on the Song of Solomon as saying, "When you consider the lovers themselves, think not of a man and a woman but of the Word and the soul."[6]

Indeed, in our relationship with God, our souls always represent the female. Equally, God, in his intimate love relationship with us, is always the one who gives the seed (male) rather than the one who receives it (female). Although many of the references to God as *he* are linguistic conventions that result from the limitations of human language, sometimes the male designation is actually the appropriate metaphor (just as some other references to God are rightly intended as female).

Of course, there is more to the seed parables, and in other places we are told that the seeds are the children of the kingdom (see Matthew 13:38). Even in these cases, however, it is quite possible that the seed refers to the same thing that it did in the previously considered parable. Indeed, just as our physical existence began as a seed, in the same way our life in Christ began as a seed—namely, the word of God. Indeed, our life in Christ began when we opened ourselves and allowed the word of God to come and produce new life within us. *You have been born anew, not of perishable but of imperishable seed, through the living and enduring word of God* (1 Peter 1:23).

47

How exactly this happens, we do not know (see Mark 4:26–27). As mysterious as the process is, however, the analogy is quite clear, and the seed that is implanted is not unlike the husband's implanting of a seed within his wife. Consequently, the transformative process whereby we are made into God's likeness seems to begin as we open ourselves to receive God's love and the supernatural life that comes with it.

This requires a certain participation on our part. As creator, God spoke the universe into existence, and we had no part in it, but the words of a lover do require the consent of the beloved. In order for that deeper creation to begin, we must choose to open ourselves and allow God's word to continue to bring about his creation within us. As God's creatures or children, we had no choice but to accept his creative love, but as his beloved, we do have a choice. We must choose to become his beloved and receive his seed. If we are to be made into the fullness of his likeness, the bringing forth of this new life requires that we first be impregnated, and that requires consent on our part. Those who have not opened themselves to God, and allowed his word to begin to create new life after his likeness, may look and act religious; they may even work miracles in Jesus' name, but, unless they have been impregnated by him, he never knew them, and they are not his beloved.

> "On that day many will say to me, 'Lord, Lord, did we not prophesy in your name, and cast out demons in your name, and do many deeds of power in your name?' Then I will declare to them, 'I never knew you; go away from me, you evildoers'" (Matthew 7:22–23).

It is difficult to interpret this passage, and in particular the word *knew*, in any other way but as a personal intimacy, as when Scripture says, *Now the man knew his wife Eve, and she conceived* (Genesis 4:1). To understand the word in any other way simply does not make sense. God knows all things. The hairs of our head are all counted, so no one escapes God's notice, but many refuse the kind of intimacy that would allow his seed to produce the fullness of life within them. God may be their creator, and even their loving Father, but they have never become his beloved because they have never received his seed in order to bring forth the new life that is after his likeness.

As our father and creator, God gave us life, over which we had no choice, but concerning the creation of a new life after his likeness, we do have a choice. In order to come into the fullness of life he has for us, we must allow him to become our lover and impregnate us with his seed. This is the ultimate union God desires: one in which he is the lover and giver of life, and we are the beloved who willingly receive that fullness of life.

The life that comes out of this intimate union will certainly resemble the God who fathered it, but, since this new life is created in us, it will also bear a striking resemblance to us as well. Thus, the Christian life that comes forth from within us looks different in every individual, while at the same time looking the same in everyone because of its resemblance to the lover who fathered it.

Interestingly, this aspect of divine love, whereby God impregnates us so that we might begin to bring forth new life, is not reciprocal. We cannot impregnate God as he impregnates us. Toward God we will always be the feminine and receptor of the seed. (The consequence of this is that we can never be God's lover, and we can never have the same kind of divine love toward him as he has toward us.) With respect to God, we will always be the beloved, having a human love that desires to acquire rather than to impart and create. Thus, if we are to be like him, and have his kind of love, it must be toward other human beings and not toward God. Although we cannot be God's lover, we can be the lovers of other human beings and have the same love for them that God has for us. We are the body of Christ, and God uses us to pass on his seed and thus impregnate others with the same words of life with which we have been impregnated.

This is the holiness God has for us, not an outward moral purity, but a God-given ability to love the unlovely and create within them the capacity to do the same. It is by this divine love for the unlovely, and the impregnating of them with words of life that they too become agents of the divine love, that the virus of the gospel spreads.

Love as Attention

The third important way that God's love is different from human love is in regard to the matter of attention. José Ortega y Gasset (1883–1955) had claimed that love was essentially a matter of attention abnormally fixed. "Falling in love, initially, is no more than this: attention abnormally fastened upon another person."[7]

His claim is that within the consciousness of the lover there is the constant presence of the beloved. This certainly seems true of the love that exists between people who are romantically "in love." Indeed, lovers are individuals who have their attention abnormally fixed upon their beloved. "For the lover, his beloved...possesses a constant presence,"[8] and occupies the lover's attention in a way that nothing else can.

In saying that "'falling in love' is a phenomenon of attention," Ortega y Gasset is referring specifically to the romantic relationship between a man and a woman, but what he describes also applies to other forms of love, and it is what we all desire in terms of being loved. The affection children desire from their parents largely involves attention, in the same way that the affection we desire in a romantic relationship largely involves attention. Even friendships, if they are to be meaningful, require that we are capable of fixing our attention on our friend, and if someone we consider a friend is unwilling to give us his or her attention, we feel we may have been mistaken in considering the person a friend in the first place.

Unfortunately, however, as much as we desire the attention of spouses, parents, or friends, human beings are not very good at fixing our attention on any one individual for very long. The attention of a normal human being is constantly changing from one object to another.[9] Because of this, we are a constant disappointment to our spouses, children, and friends. My wife's disappointment in me, as a lover, usually focuses on my lack of attention. "You're not here" is her complaint. And although I try to assure her that I was listening and can even repeat what she said, her complaint is still true. I may have been listening, but I was not attentive. My wife knows that to be truly loved is a matter of attention, and she is frustrated by my lack of attention. Small children seem instinctively to know the same thing and evidence it by clamoring to their mothers, "Watch me!"

Of course, parents disappoint children, just as spouses disappoint each other, because human attention is fleeting even concerning the things we love most. Indeed, if a lover is one who fixes his attention on his beloved, then the vast majority of human beings make poor lovers. Fortunately, our desire to be loved by one who gives us extraordinary attention is not completely frustrated, since God is quite different from human beings in this regard. Because of his omnipresent and omniscient nature, God is able to give us attention in ways that other human beings are not. Unlike other human beings who constantly fail us in this regard, God says, *"My eyes and my heart will be there for all time"* (2 Chronicles 7:16). Indeed, his *"eyes will be open and [his] ears attentive"* (2 Chronicles 7:15), and *as an eagle...hovers over its young* (Deuteronomy 32:11), he will attend to us as *the apple of his eye* (see Deuteronomy 32:10 and Zechariah 2:8).

It is his omnipresent and omniscient nature that makes God the supreme lover and the only one who can truly satisfy our desire for attention. Of course, the attention he gives us is not mechanical and the result merely of his omniscient and omnipresent nature. It is rather the result of his will. His nature makes him aware of the whole of his creation, but he has chosen to fix his attention upon us as the centerpiece of that creation. Our potential to be made into divine lovers after the image of his son is what brings us into special focus.

Interestingly, this attention, which is an essential aspect of God's love toward us, is also an aspect of the kind of love that we are to have toward God. Although existing in an imperfect degree in human beings, our love for God is largely a matter of attention just as his love toward us is largely a matter of attention. Thus, unlike the desire to impregnate and bring forth offspring in the beloved, attention is a characteristic of divine love that is reciprocal. Indeed, we love God to the extent that God is in all our thoughts. Just as children measure the love of their parents by the amount and quality of the attention they give them, and wives measure the love of their husbands by their attention, we can measure our love toward God by attention as well. It is good that we consider the measure of our attention toward God, for when we realize how minuscule our attention is in comparison to his worthiness, and likewise how perfect his attention despite our unworthiness, we should be humbled and brought to a correct perspective of God and ourselves. Only from such a perspective do we see our true sin and what separates us from God. If the first and great commandment is to love God, and love—at least the kind of love we are capable of having toward God—is largely a matter of attention, then our great sin (perhaps our only sin) is our lack of attention toward God. That is, our sin is the fact that our attention is abnormally fixed on things other than God. This concept of sin is the focus of the next chapter.

Questions for Reflection

1. Is human love different from divine love? Explain.
2. What is the highest form of love?
3. What is the difference between acquisitive love and creative love?

4

The Sermon on the Mount
and the Concept of Sin

We all have a concept of sin. Many of us believe that God has somehow implanted that idea in us so that we would have no excuse for doing evil. There may be some truth to this, but it is certainly not the whole story. Our concept of sin is also enormously influenced by cultural forces. Our concepts are always convoluted, and although we may have been given some universal sentiments of right or wrong, or some sort of innate sense of what is praiseworthy or shameful, human forces within culture and history enormously shape those concepts. It is similar with our concept of sin.

Even where our concept of sin is shaped by biblical influences, those influences do not generally go much beyond the "shalt nots" and warnings of the Law. We tend to interpret adultery, stealing, murder, or bearing false witness as standard rules for avoiding harm to others. We perceive that, perhaps for the sake of social order or concern for human beings, God merely forbids us to do harm to others. Our culture has also led us to believe that any violation of the commandments will anger God and cause God to reject us—even punish us. Ten Commandment placards at public courthouses seem to suggest that harming others will result in rejection by society and God.

But if you will not obey me, and do not observe all these commandments, if you spurn my statutes, and abhor my ordinances, so that you will not observe all my commandments, and you break my covenant, I in turn will do this to you: I will bring terror on you, consumption and fever that waste the eyes and cause life to pine away. You shall sow your seed in vain, for your enemies shall eat it. I will set my face against you, and you shall be struck down by your enemies; your foes shall rule over you, and you shall flee though no one pursues you (Leviticus 26:14–17).

Preserve others and serve God, or else!

However, the greater truth—the fuller truth (or fulfillment of truth) that Jesus reveals—is a much more comprehensive notion of sin. Jesus' understanding of sin is one that is very different from our accepted, popular (cultural) understanding. It is a radical notion of sin in that it addresses sin at its root. The Sermon on the Mount provides a great example.

The Sermon on the Mount

In the Sermon on the Mount, Jesus sets forth a standard for righteousness—and consequently a standard for sin—that is very different from what anyone had previously imagined. It is certainly very different from what Moses had set forth. Of course, as we have seen, Jesus is quick to say that he is not doing away with the law but rather fulfilling it (see Matthew 5:17). When we hear what he says, however, it becomes obvious that the "fulfillment of the law" was merely a first step toward a right relationship with God. The Law (Torah) taught us that we were not to murder, but Jesus tells us that we are not even to be angry with our brother (see Matthew 5:21–22). The Law told us not to commit adultery, but Jesus tells us that we are not even to have lustful thoughts (see Matthew 5:27–28).

Separated From God

At first glance, Jesus' law appears as merely an amplified version of the ancient Law—indeed, a law even more impossible to keep than the Law of Moses. However, such a law could hardly be considered "good news." Furthermore, when we examine the Sermon on the Mount, we find something very different from a moral law or code.

Jesus tells us that we are not to make oaths (see Matthew 5:27–28), and we are not to seek retribution—that is, justice (see Matthew 5:27–28). Rather, we are to love our enemies (see Matthew 5:43–44). And when we give alms, pray, or fast, we are to do it in a way so as not to be noticed (see Matthew 6:1–18). Finally, he tells us that we are not to seek earthly treasure, worry, or make judgments concerning others (see Matthew 6:19–7:2). What a strange set of dictates. They are not moral in nature, nor do they immediately seem to fit into some other obvious category. So what are they?

Jesus' condemnations in the Sermon on the Mount are nothing like our typical interpretation of sin, because we think of sin as some immoral behavior that causes God to withdraw from us. Jesus, however, knows that God does not withdraw from us but we withdraw from him. So I suggest that what is set forth in the Sermon on the Mount is what Jesus sees as our real sin—that which truly separates us from God and for which we need to repent. That is, we attach ourselves to the false gods of this world in order to find life and meaning in them. It seems that what Jesus is doing in the Sermon on the Mount is pointing out all the things that give meaning and motivation to so many, but in the end are disappointing sources of life. Sin, then, is not so much a matter of harming others as it is a matter of trying to find life and meaning apart from God.

God's Suffering

Our sin is also the source of God's suffering. It is like the suffering of a father or mother who sees their child choosing a life that is so much less than what they desire for him or her. It is not, as we so often imagine, that sin is an offense to God's divine ego. Rather sin is that which grieves the heart of God because he desires so much more for his children than what they choose for themselves.

It is hard for us to realize our true sin, because we do not know God in his fullness. When, however, we see him face to face and see who he really is, we will realize how we have rejected his presence and the things with which he wishes to bless us. Equally, upon coming to know God, we will also realize how much destruction we had brought upon ourselves and others by doing what seemed good in *our* eyes. If only we had eyes that truly see and ears that truly hear.

So this is our sin: that God is not in all of our thoughts and we are not directed by him in all of our actions. Instead, our time and attention are fixed upon hosts of other things—our false gods. Despite some of our best public efforts at church (or even on the streets or in the privacy of our homes), we find ourselves drawing life and meaning from the false gods of which Jesus warns us.

In the Sermon on the Mount, Jesus tells us that it is not the act of murder that separates us from God. We separate ourselves from God long before, when we become possessed by the spirit of anger rather than God. We sin, and separate ourselves from God, when the source of our energy—the thing that motivates us—is not God but something that keeps us from an awareness of God and his presence in our lives.

> *"You have heard that it was said to those of ancient times, 'You shall not murder'; and 'whoever murders shall be liable to judgment.' But I say to you that if you are angry with your brother or sister, you will be liable to judgment; and if you insult a brother or sister, you will be liable to the council; and if you say, 'You fool,' you will be liable to the hell of fire"* (Matthew 5:21–22).

For many of us, anger is our source of energy and life; it fuels us and is a source of strength. Athletes and other competitors often find strength and motivation in anger, but Jesus tells us that God alone is to be our source of strength and life.

Separated by Infidelity

In the Sermon on the Mount, Jesus says, *"You have heard that it was said, 'You shall not commit adultery.' But I say to you that everyone who looks at a woman with lust has already committed adultery with her in his heart"* (Matthew 5:27–28). Society suggests that if we do not harm others—in this case, if we do not actually commit adultery—we have not actually sinned. Jesus, on the other hand, tells us that our sin rests in our thoughts of adultery. There may be several reasons for this, but certainly one is that imagined infidelity provides energy and direction for our lives in a way that should be reserved for God alone. Thus, it is not that the act of adultery so displeases God that he turns away from us in disgust, but rather we turn away from God as soon as our imagination focuses on our erotic desires rather than God. The popularity of pornography is evidence of the fact that sexuality often becomes our god—not just when we commit adultery, but when we allow the thoughts of such things to take hold of our attention and begin to direct our lives.

Make No Oath

The third thing that Jesus mentions in the Sermon on the Mount is that we are not to make oaths. Moses had given prohibitions against the breaking of oaths (see Deuteronomy 7:8 and Numbers 30:2), but now Jesus tells us we should make no oaths at all.

> *"Again, you have heard that it was said to those of ancient times, 'You shall not swear falsely, but carry out the vows you have made to the Lord.' But I say to you, Do not swear at all, either by heaven, for it is the throne of God, or by the earth, for it is his footstool, or by Jerusalem, for it is the city of the great King. And do not swear by your head, for you cannot make one hair white or black"* (Matthew 5:33–36).

Pledging allegiance to anything other than God would have been perceived as idolatry by the first-century Church. Our culture today is quite different, and we believe that it is noble to keep our word even when our oaths cause us to end up in ungodly allegiances. Of course, breaking any oath is a problem as well. Thus, in Matthew 5:34, Jesus tells us to promise our commitment to no one or no thing but God. He is warning us not to replace God with other gods to whom we pledge allegiance. Jesus knows that oaths can serve as a source of strength apart from God. We boast to others and take pride in giving our word, as if there was power in our words and their ability to control circumstances. Jesus tells us that we are not in control over the circumstances of our lives and thus to swear to do this or that is a false witness and a claim to power that we do not possess. We would like to think that we are people of our word and that our word is enough to motivate us to do what we have sworn. If we are honest with ourselves, however, we realize that we deceive ourselves in believing that there is power in our oaths. Jesus reminds us that in our human capacity we cannot even *"make one hair white or black."* Of course, we love the illusion of power within ourselves and therefore swear oaths, as if we were able to will to do this or that out of the power of our word. Therein lies our sin, and we are separated from God as we attempt to find power in ourselves rather than him.

Retribution and Enemies

> *"You have heard that it was said, 'An eye for eye and tooth for tooth.' But I say to you, Do not resist an evildoer. But if anyone strikes you on the right cheek, turn the other also"* (Matthew 5:38–39).

The Mosaic Law allowed for retribution, but it seems that it was hardly God's ultimate standard. What Jesus reveals is that retribution is ultimately a source of sin in that it separates us from God and the fullness of life he has for us. Indeed, many of us focus on the sins of others and find energy and motivation through retribution. The life that Jesus reveals does not need retribution for motivation. With God alone as our source of energy and strength, we can turn the other cheek, because our strength does not come from our desire for retribution. Rather our strength comes from a God who is willing to pay for the injustice of others.

The next idea set forth in the Sermon on the Mount is a commandment that the people of his day were not ready to receive, just as we are still not ready to receive it today. Jesus says,

> *"You have heard that it was said, 'You shall love your neighbor and hate your enemy.' But I say to you, Love your enemies and pray for those who persecute you, so that you may be children of your Father in heaven"* (Matthew 5:43–45).

This is not merely a difficult commandment; it is an *a priori* impossible command. Enemies are by definition people we do not love. If we love our enemies, the idea of an enemy loses its meaning. Is it possible to love your enemy? Perhaps Jesus could ask us not to take revenge upon our enemies or maybe even not to hate them, but to *love* them seems beyond the realm of what we are capable. Indeed, the only way that it is possible is if we are connected to an incredibly loving and forgiving God as the source of our being and identity. The love of God, and our connection to it, is what makes possible the commandment to love our enemies, and this love is what is behind everything Jesus says in the Sermon on the Mount and elsewhere.

Almsgiving, Prayer, and Fasting

Giving to the needy is to be done in such a way that you do not gain recognition. Thus, it is not enough that we give, but we must give with the right attitude—that is, without a desire for recognition (see Matthew 6:1). This may seem strange since previously Jesus said, *"Let your light shine before others, so that they may see your good works and give glory to your Father in heaven"* (Matthew 5:16). But your light will not shine if it is not authentic. Thus giving with the intent to be seen cannot be considered a "good work." Indeed, such self-indulgent almsgiving brings us glory rather than God. The real problem with giving for the sake of recognition is that we are seeking an identity founded on prestige and reputation rather than our relationship with God. We often seek to be made into an image of human greatness rather than the image and likeness of God.

There is a similar situation with the religious practices of prayer and fasting. As with almsgiving, prayer and fasting are to be done in secret so that no one but God knows. It is not enough that we pray and fast, but we must do it without being motivated by a desire for reputation or esteem. Our sin is that we reject the identity God gives us in order to find favor among human beings. We seek a human identity rather than who we are in God. Such sin separates us from a God who desires to be our ultimate and only source of worth and identity.

Attachment to Worldly Things

Jesus then warns us concerning our attachment to earthly treasures.

> *"Do not store up for yourselves treasures on earth, where moth and rust consume and where thieves break in and steal; but store up for yourselves treasures in heaven"* (Matthew 6:19–20).

We easily become attached to the things of this world and very easily they, rather than God, become the things from which we attempt to draw life. Many people, especially successful people, draw their energy from their treasure and the things they have accomplished in this life. Jesus tells us that such treasures are a fleeting source of worth and we will soon be disappointed if we put our hope in them rather than God.

Have Faith

And when he got into the boat, his disciples followed him. A great storm arose on the sea, so great that the boat was being swamped by the waves; but he was asleep. And they went and woke him up, saying, "Lord, save us! We are perishing!" And he said to them, "Why are you afraid, you of little faith?" Then he got up and rebuked the winds and the sea; and there was a great calm (Matthew 8:23–27).

Jesus tells us not to worry (see Matthew 6:25). Certainly being frightened is not a sin, but as we allow what scares us to dwell in our hearts, and we nurture our worries, we separate ourselves from the assurance that God offers. Anxiety is not the kind of faith to which Jesus is calling us. When we are anxious about many things, our attention is not on God. With worry at the center of our being, God cannot be present in all of our thoughts and, consequently, our worries overcome us.

Do Not Judge

Jesus says, *"Do not judge"* (Matthew 7:1). But judging is what we most want to do. Our desire to have a standard to judge the saved from the unsaved, the godly from the ungodly, and the moral from the immoral forms the basis of much contemporary theology. We mistakenly think that we can discern good from evil. According to Jesus, however, our human limitations prevent us from judging others (and ourselves) as God judges us. Therefore we cannot adequately distinguish the wheat from the weeds (see Matthew 13:24–30). Indeed, if God's true standard for righteousness is being revealed in the Sermon on the Mount, our popular concepts of sin and righteousness must be so far off that any judgments we make about others are likely to be in error. We are certainly lost in our own human conceptualization of right and wrong, but we are not hopelessly lost, for now comes the good news.

Ask, and It Will Be Given to You

Following the impossible standard that Jesus has just set forth, he now reveals the good news that all we need do is to ask and it will be given to us.

> *"Ask, and it will be given to you; search, and you will find; knock, and the door will be opened for you. For everyone who asks receives, and everyone who searches finds, and for everyone who knocks, the door will be opened"* (Matthew 7:7–8).

In light of all that Jesus has said, it seems obvious that what we need to ask for is that God would give us a spirit of repentance so that we might turn from these false gods and find the God who is the true lover of our soul. In this world we will always face false gods and false sources of life that subtly separate us from the fullness of life that God has for us. These are the things that possess us and keep our attention focused on them rather than God. Therefore, what we need is a grace that will allow us not to tire of repentance. What we need is to turn continually away from these false sources of life in order that we might find our identity in God alone. God is willing to give us the ability to turn again and again from those things that promise but deliver so little, if we simply ask. It seems obvious from all Jesus has said that we need to ask for repentance to fill our soul and to live in a constant state of turning back to him and away from all those things that so easily entrap us and keep us from drawing our strength and energy—our life and meaning—from God alone. Remaining in God's presence is essentially a matter of simply turning back to him every time we find our attention abnormally fixed on things that divert attention away from God. Thus, we find God's presence and remain in it through repentance.

Our Relationship With God

We can easily be kept from living in a state of repentance by our cultural concept of sin. Our cultural concept interprets sin as merely a moral evil and, therefore, many of us see little reason for repentance. Because we have a wrong idea of sin, we have a wrong idea of repentance as well. If, however, our real sin is that our hearts are prone to wander and seek life and meaning apart from God, then we need to live in a constant state of turning back to God every time we find ourselves looking to those false sources of life. Every time we do so, we are renewed with an awareness of God's forgiveness and grace.

The good news of the gospel is that God is not calling us to obey a moral law involving endless requirements. He is calling us to a relationship, and all we need to do to maintain that relationship is to turn from the false gods that surround us and so easily engulf us. We do not need to find God, he finds us. We, however, only become aware of having been found when we turn from those false gods and idols that capture our attention and keep us from an awareness of God and the fullness of life he has for us.

Of course, in order to turn from the things of this world that so easily capture us and hold us in their sway, we must see a need to do so. Most people are content with the gods of this world. They like the life that comes from their lust, anger, and even worry. They are happy with earthy treasure and the reputation they have taken so long to acquire. Wealth, power, and prestige afford them social standing and thus they find meaning and purpose for their lives. Ungodly comforts define them, and they see no reason to turn away from such things. But Jesus tells us at the beginning of the Sermon on the Mount that the truly fortunate or blessed ones *"are the poor in spirit"* (Matthew 5:3). Jesus came *"to bring good news to the poor"* (Luke 4:18). Consequently, if the poor are the fortunate ones for whom Jesus has good news, the rich must not be fortunate—for them, what Jesus says is not good news. True, the rich may enjoy their wealth, power, and prestige while the poor have nothing in this world, but in their poverty the poor have little else as a source of identity but God alone.

Thus, the truly fortunate ones are the poor in spirit who lack a rich identity in the things of this world, for it is in detachment from the things of this world that we can attach ourselves to a true identity in God. Unfortunately, most of us are not poor in spirit. We feel good about ourselves and are proud of how much we have accomplished, all the good we have done, and all the evil we have avoided. But if we consider what Jesus says, we should see that we have stored up treasures on earth, sought the approval of humanity, and proudly stood in our own judgments. Truly, the poor in spirit are the blessed ones, for they have nothing but God as the source of their identity and self-worth. They are certainly freer from many of the sources of the false identity that the rest of us find so difficult to escape. The beatitudes go on to say that the blessed ones

> *"...are those who mourn, for they will be comforted.*
> *"Blessed are the meek, for they will inherit the earth.*
> *"Blessed are those who hunger and thirst for righteousness,*
>   *for they will be filled.*
> *"Blessed are the merciful, for they will be shown mercy.*
> *"Blessed are the pure in heart, for they will see God"*
>   (Matthew 5:4–8).

Only when we mourn the loss of all that others hold dear do we find the God who is the only true source of comfort and joy. Equally, it is not the self-righteous who are meek but those who realize their sin and separation from God. They alone *"hunger and thirst for righteousness"* (Matthew 5:6), for those who are satisfied and content with their own righteousness have no need to mourn or hunger and thirst. The only truly blessed ones are those who are full of mercy, for they will be shown mercy (see Matthew 5:7). Our general understanding of this verse is that God shows mercy in exchange for us having shown mercy to others, but here *merciful* means to be full of mercy. The only ones who are truly full of mercy are those who have seen their great need for mercy and cry out to God. It is only those who have received mercy who are truly able to extend it to others. Finally, our ability to see God is conditioned upon our ability to repent and turn from all those other gods who stand in the way and prevent us from seeing the God who Jesus reveals. This is the purity of heart of which Jesus speaks—that we would be pure, having a single source of life and identity in God.

The Beatitudes, and what follows them in the Sermon on the Mount, are linked in that the latter explains why the poor in spirit, the mournful, meek souls who hunger for righteousness and mercy are blessed. If we accept what Jesus is setting forth as God's true standard, we realize our poverty of spirit and our need for mercy. In light of what Jesus says, a humble state of repentance, in which we seek God's mercy, is the only blessed place. Of course, those who do not accept what Jesus is setting forth as God's ultimate standard but are confident that they can achieve their own righteousness by following some set of religious principles or practices, are not the poor-spirited, meek, and mournful souls who Jesus tells us are the blessed ones.

In Jesus' day, the Pharisees probably kept the Mosaic Law better than any group of Jews who had ever lived. They took great pride in their observance and they believed that they were living according to God's ultimate standard. What Jesus reveals, however, is a deeper spiritual life of faith. The Pharisees resisted and wished to stay where their identity was well founded. They were good at keeping the law, but Jesus was calling them to a deeper communion with God through repentance and radical faith in the mercy and love of God.

We continually find ourselves to be something other than poor spirited, meek, and mournful, but, like the Pharisee, we cling to our doctrinal beliefs or good behavior that we are sure will be our salvation. The French theologian François Fénelon (1651–1715) beautifully describes the pharisaical condition to which we all so easily fall prey.

> The Pharisees were religious reformers who carried out every detail of the Law. Their outward religion would dazzle you, but inside they were blinded by their own self-righteousness.

> The tax collectors were social outcasts, hated by all. Jesus tells a story about the tax collector and the Pharisee. The tax collector is ashamed of his sin. The Pharisee is proud of his virtue. But God prefers the sinner, overwhelmed by his wretchedness, who trusts in God alone.

> The Pharisee is much more common than you think. Many Christians try to lead "good, Christian lives" and are proud of themselves for it. They may pray, tithe, and lead moral lives, but inside they are attached to their own ability to live the Christian life.

> You have hidden (or not so hidden) pride at your own strength. You take pleasure in seeing yourself as strong and good and righteous. But whom are you trusting, and whom are you looking at in all of this? Yourself! You want to know the good feeling that comes with being right with God. You need to empty

yourself, not fill yourself up. Follow God by the dim torch of faith, not by the light of your own understanding and abilities. Do not be proud of your apparent ability to live the Christian life. Your ability to do that will soon prove to be an illusion. Trust in God alone.[1]

The Christian life of faith is not an absolute certainty in this or that doctrine but rather a hope in the greatness of God's mercy. After all, *faith is the assurance of things hoped for* (Hebrews 11:1). That type of faith can only come about when we abandon our personal hopes and live in that blessed place of repentance and trust in the mercy of God. Such is the narrow gate that Jesus tells us is the only way to eternal life (Matthew 7:13–14).

Based on what Jesus says in the Sermon on the Mount and elsewhere in the gospels, we get a concept of sin that is certainly different than our general cultural concept. According to our inherited presuppositions, sin is a moral evil that somehow offends God and causes him to turn his back on us. However, Jesus tells us that it is we who have turned our backs on God to seek other sources of life and identity.

If it is true, however, that sin is not a matter of moral evil, then what is evil? How is evil different from sin, and what is God's response to it?

Questions for Reflection

1. What do you think Jesus means by sin, and how does his understanding seem to be different from what most human cultures have understood to be sin?
2. Do you accept the conventional notion of sin as behavioral, or is sin more a matter of the heart?
3. Does God separate himself from us because of sin?

5

A Better Understanding
of Good and Evil

If we reconstruct our concept of sin in order to better reflect Jesus'
teachings, other concepts will change as well. Since our concepts
are not isolated but interwoven, a change of one concept creates
changes in other concepts, especially those that are closely related. Two
such concepts are those of good and evil, the focus of this chapter. Our
hope is to rethink them in ways that will make them more compatible
with, and more conducive to, authentic Christian living.

Although sin and evil are not synonymous, evil is rooted in sin. If
sin is both what separates us from God and what offends God, then,
based on what Jesus says, things like abortion and adultery might better
be seen, not as sins, but as the evils that result from sin. That is because
long before we commit adultery or have an abortion, we offend God by
separating ourselves from him.

Our cultural understanding of sin defines God as one who tolerates
our bad or wayward thoughts as long as we stop short of acting on
those thoughts. We imagine that our thoughts are not harmful because
we want to see ourselves as sinless, or at least less sinful than others.
The main point of the gospels, however, is to show us that sin is in our
hearts long before evil acts are committed. Thus, we are all sinners in
need of repentance, not for our evil deeds but for our wayward hearts.

Sin does not always look evil in itself, but it leads to evil. As seen in the last chapter, sin involves our choosing sources of life and meaning other than God. Idolatry is our great sin—our only sin. Clinging to other gods in an attempt to find meaning and identity keeps us from God and all of the blessing he has for us. This is our sin and what causes God to suffer.

Evil, on the other hand, is the destruction that follows from our sin or the fact that God is no longer in all of our thoughts. Once we are no longer in God's presence and under his sovereign hand, we open ourselves to destruction rather creation. Since our sin or separation from God stifles the creation that God wants to continue within us, evil sets in as the privation or absence of God's ongoing creation.

Augustine uses something very much like this to explain the problem of evil. That is, how could an all-good and all-powerful God create a world that is full of evil? Augustine's explanation was that God did not create evil at all. Rather God created us with only good desires (or what Augustine refers to as *loves*), and equally God only created good things to satisfy those desires. Of course, our God-given desire for friendship was intended to be satisfied by our neighbors, and our God-given desire for sex by our spouse. Evil and destruction enter the world when we decide to use our neighbor to satisfy our desire for sex. The reason we make such a choice, however, is that our ultimate desire is not being satisfied by God. Our ultimate desire for a meaningful and purposeful life can only be satisfied by God. When we attempt to satisfy that desire with anything but God, it affects all of our other choices. When God is not in that right place of providing us with meaning and purpose for our lives, other things quickly take his place. Our lust, anger, worry, or desire for earthly treasure and reputation quickly fill the gap, and destruction or evil enters our lives instead of the fullness of life that God has for us.

Evil is a byproduct of sin and not sin itself. For example, the act of abortion—the death of human life—is an evil. The sin occurs long before the act of abortion. The sin that leads to abortion occurs when our worry, concern for our reputation, or considerations of earthly treasure occupy us and remove us from an awareness of God's presence and all that he has for us. This sin creates a godless vacuum in which evil emerges as the destruction that opposes God's creation. Similarly, taking innocent life through murder or war is an evil that results from the sin of ignoring God's presence in creation. The antecedent to murder is our sinful worship of self-proclaimed, tribal gods—such as monetary gain or political strength—that allow for slaughter in the name of jealously, greed, patriotism, or anything else that claims to be of great enough value to consume our lives. Thus, evil is the consequence or outward sign of sin. Just as the sacrament is an outward sign of a spiritual death and resurrection, or tithing an outward sign of the spiritual reality of our trust in God and his provision, so, too, is evil an outward sign of the spiritual reality of our separation from God.

Most people conceive of sin and evil as synonymous. If sin is synonymous with evil, we can imagine that we do not sin or offend God since we refrain from so many of the evils of which others are guilty. We all seem to want some other way to God apart from his mercy and forgiveness, and if sin and evil are equivalent, we can imagine ourselves as good and therefore loved by God because of our goodness rather than his mercy. With the much broader notion of sin that Jesus sets forth, however, we should realize that sin—that which separates us from God—is our preference to have our lives shaped and defined by our reputation, worries, lusts, and earthly treasures rather than by God. If we heed what Jesus tells us, we will see that we are all sinners and we can only maintain a relationship with God through his mercy and forgiveness.

Despite the fact that sin and evil are causally connected, it is important to understand them as distinctly different, and it is equally important to understand God's reaction to them as distinctly different. God's response to sin, or our rejection of him, is to love us always, even if it causes him great pain and suffering—even death on a cross. Unlike human beings who typically respond to rejection by striking out in retaliation, God's response is to bear the rejection and offer forgiveness in order to restore the relationship.

For Christ also suffered for sins once for all, the righteous for the unrighteous, in order to bring you to God (1 Peter 3:18).

As in any relationship, it is impossible for the sinner—the one responsible for the destruction of the relationship—to force forgiveness. The sinner is helpless without the victim's willingness to forgive. God's desire is always for restoration, and since we are the ones who have broken the relationship through our choice of lesser gods, restoration can only come through God's forgiveness. Of course, many reject God's attempt at restoration and spurn his forgiveness. They trust their self-appraisal that they have done little evil in their lives compared to others, and they imagine that only the most grievous evils offend God and destroy our relationship with him. But as we have seen, our relationship with God is not based on the good that we do, nor is it destroyed by the sins we commit. It is based on God's goodness and the fact that he is willing and able to forgive us for having rejected him and the life that he has for us.

Although God responds to sin with suffering and forgiveness in the hope that we would repent and turn back to him, that is not always his response to evil. Of course, God is slow to respond to evil even when there is no repentance and the destruction that is evil abounds. God often permits the evil that follows from our separation from him to continue, knowing that it is often the manifestation of evil that produces repentance. We often turn from our false gods only when we see the destruction that follows our attachment to them and our consequent separation from God.

God, however, will only allow evil that he can turn to his purpose. God is the Lord of all and, as such, he is Lord over evil. He can cause good to emerge from the evil we create through sin. If, however, the evil that follows from our separation from God becomes so pervasive that it is no longer conducive to repentance and it can no longer be turned to good, God, in his infinite mercy, will eventually bring it to an end. God allows the weeds and the wheat to grow until the end of time (see Matthew 13:30). Until then, God *"makes his sun rise on the evil and on the good, and sends rain on the righteous and on the unrighteous"* (Matthew 5:45), providing every opportunity for good to flourish through repentance and restored relationship. At the end of time, however, all the powers of evil—even death itself—will be destroyed (see 1 Corinthians 15:24–28). God does everything out of love for his creation, and eventually his creation triumphs over all the evil and destruction that oppose it.

Morality and Transformation

A God who is slow to anger and always merciful (see Exodus 34:6) tolerates a great deal of evil, leaving us with the impression of a God who does not provide much motivation to do good and avoid evil. Why should we avoid sin and evil if God loves us in spite of our actions? We would rather have a god that is cloaked as a moralist, a large Leviathan capable of providing and enforcing moral order. The God of the gospel, however, does not seem to be interested in being the enforcer of moral order. Jesus condemns the Pharisees despite their keeping the Law, and he promises the thief on the cross paradise despite his crime. Jesus condemns and rewards the wrong people because God's first priority is not moral order. This does not mean that God is against morality. He does oppose evil, but his opposition to evil emerges from his love for creation and, in particular, his desire for creation to continue within us, transforming us into the divine image. God's ultimate purpose for our lives is not merely our obedience to a moral law; rather, God desires our transformation into the likeness of his Son.

Transformation is very different from obedience and morality. Obedience to moral law allows us to remain who we are. Transformation requires a continual process of death and resurrection. It is not about becoming a good person but about becoming a new creation—an ever-new creation.

Of course, the Christian life does involve morality. As we experience transformation, we come to do good and avoid evil, but that is a byproduct of transformation and not its goal. Christian morality is radical and attacks evil at its root. At the root of all moral evil is self-interest, and where self-interest rules, evil abounds. By contrast, life abounds where God rules. The Christian solution to moral evil is to bring an end to the autonomous self at the root of sin and bring forth a new life *in* God.

True conversion is a slow process by which we sin less and less because we no longer live on our own accord, *but it is Christ who lives in [us]* (Galatians 2:20). Indeed, Christian life can be painful, like death itself, but it is through such self-denial, or death, that we come to live, not in the false self we create for ourselves by identifying with worldly things, but in the god of Abraham, Isaac, and Jacob.

To be "in" God, of course, is not as water is "in" a glass; rather, "in God" implies being "in relationship," such as when someone is "in" love. In order for us to live in God, or, as Paul so often says, "in Christ," we must not live in the false self that takes its identity and life from all of the things that Jesus warns against in the Sermon on the Mount and elsewhere. This false self, whose identity is founded in the things of this world, must die in order for our relationship with God to be the basis for our identity.

We must found our identity upon the fact that we are God's beloved daughters and sons. We were God's creation before we did anything right or wrong, and he loves us because we are his. God does not love us because of the greatness of our prayers or almsgiving, nor does he love our ability to keep our oaths or make good judgments. These are the things that make other people love us, but God is not like other people. As a matter of fact, these things, which are often the very reason that others love us, are the very things that keep us from God. They keep us from God because they capture our attention and cause our conscience to be focused on them rather than on God.

If we form an identity in the things of this world, we are cut off from communion with God. Once our attention is centered on the things of this world as our source of meaning and we draw our identity from those things of which Jesus warns, we lose sight of our status as beloved children of God. By contrast, when our identity is in God, we live in the real self, or what Paul refers to as the *spirit*. When we live in the spirit, God is our source of life and meaning and we wish to commune with him constantly.

Jesus wishes for us to live as he lived, whereby our thoughts and actions—indeed, our hearts—are fashioned by God. He did not identify with, nor allow himself to be occupied by, those things of which he speaks in the Sermon on the Mount. Instead he lived his life in a constant awareness that he was the beloved Son of God. He tells us to follow him and live in that same relationship.

Sin and righteousness are essentially a question of belonging. Do we belong to God or to the world? Our natural tendency is to gravitate toward a worldly identity. Living in the spirit occurs when we repent and turn from the false gods that draw us away from God and the identity he has for us—a process that must occur again and again. Through repentance we continually re-found our identity in God. This is what it means to live in the spirit. Ultimately, our spirit is who we are at the core of our being. By contrast, the false self is the illusory self that is created by all of the false gods to whom we so easily give ourselves. The false self is not directed by God, nor is God the object of its worship. The false self is enmeshed with all those things that cloud a dynamic relationship with God.

Unless we are raised in isolation from the world, our false self is all we have and therefore our first encounter with God is an encounter between God and our false self. In fact, until we actually accept God in our hearts—and then usually long after—the false self (or who we think we are or pretend to be) is the only self we know. Furthermore, our first encounters with God commonly produce a sense of grandeur that inflates the false self beyond its normal state. We may imagine that there must be something particularly wonderful about us to attract the attention of such a great God. This is an understandable reaction, but it makes it impossible to see the true greatness of God's love. In order to truly know God, we must know ourselves. Our true reality is not who we pretend to be or who we try to convince ourselves and others to believe we are. We are not our reputation, our good works, or accomplishments. Nor are we anything else that we believe gives us value and makes us worthy of love. There is nothing in us that makes us worthy of God's love except that we are his creation—his beloved daughters and sons. In order to live out of this true self, and thus know God and the true nature of his love, the false self must be exposed. Without seeing the false self as an illusion, we can easily continue to think that God's love for us is a response to something beautiful within us, rather than because of something beautiful within God. The truth is that God loves us despite our false pretenses and not because of them.

For most of us, we only come to realize the illusory nature of the flesh or false self through the rejection that is so much a part of this world. Through the experience of rejection and suffering we realize that we have been living an illusion. With our rejection and suffering the base of our identity is shaken. When we lose our earthly treasure and reputation and our judgments prove wrong, we suffer and experience rejection. But with suffering, we often come to understand how we have been fooling ourselves. With the destruction of the false self we are open to finding an identity in God.

Of course, some individuals react in a very different way to rejection and suffering. Many hold fast to the illusion of the false self to the end. Their suffering and rejection embitter them, and they see the destruction of the false self as the end of all they have ever known or loved. Instead of finding themselves and God through their suffering, they feel destroyed by it.

Still others, who experience suffering and rejection in childhood before they have a chance to develop a false self, may have yet another reaction. For them suffering and rejection can often produce a negative false identity that makes them believe that no one, including God, could ever possibly love them. In such cases, the false self that develops is one that sees itself as so dejected that a genuine love experience with God or anyone else is extremely difficult to imagine.

Even for those who do avoid these two extremes and allow the death of the false self to bring them into a new identity in God, there is always the danger of falling back into the false self and reestablishing an identity based on worldly reputation, earthly treasure, or one's ability to make good judgments and keep their word. In fact, falling back is much more than a danger; it is typically a constant reality in which we find ourselves. Thus, as we have said before, in order to stay in a right relationship with God, there is need for constant repentance or turning away from those false sources of life that so easily entrap us.

The Nature of the Good

Having reconceptualized our ideas of sin and evil, we also need to say something about our idea of the good. Many would like to believe that we possess a God-given notion of the good, and certainly there may be some truth to the idea that some things are almost universally seen as morally praiseworthy. But apart from a strictly moral sense, and in terms of those things that we see as good and which we pursue in the hope of finding meaning and purpose for our lives, our idea of what is good certainly does vary enormously over time and from culture to culture. From one individual to the next, we find great variation concerning what we perceive to be good.

Even if we were to agree universally that things that lead to life and creation are good, and things that lead to death and destruction are evil, we are still left with the question of what leads to life and what leads to death? This seems to require a wisdom that escapes us, for even if we trust the wisdom that science offers and we reduce our cholesterol, exercise, and do not smoke (therein prolonging our physical life), we are left wondering whether the relationships and careers we pursue will bring life or death to our souls. In our dealings with other people, what are we to do to produce life rather than death in ourselves and others?

Plato claimed that we all have a desire for what is good or at least what we believe to be good. Few of us, however, truly have excellent lives simply because we do not have an adequate idea of what is truly good. This is as true for Christians as for anyone else. Indeed, although we may make the pretense of the good life, it should be obvious to us that our idea of the good life and God's idea are very different. If you have trouble believing this, consider the fact that an all-wise God, who we believe has a perfect knowledge of the good, chose for his son a life that we would never willingly choose for ourselves or our children. Obviously, if God is good and only does good, he has a very different idea of what is good.

The college where I teach was originally a missionary college. The first graduating class in the nineteenth century produced five graduates. They all went into the mission field and all died within a few years. The college never puts that fact in the catalog—it's not a good way to recruit students. Why? Because our idea of what would be good for our lives is very different from what God thinks is good. For his own son, God chose a short and difficult life that led to a painful death. God chose this for his son because he knew what was ultimately good in a way that we do not. We choose the lives we do because of our own immediate pleasure and our ill-conceived idea of what is good. We tend to waste away our lives because we cannot get beyond our ill-conceived idea of the good and confess to God that we do not know what is good and that we need his wisdom and direction in that regard.

Our ill-conceived notion of the good is at the base of much of what we call Christianity. We spend much time and effort either trying to become good so that God would love us, or trying to have God bless us so that our lives might be good and that we might love our lives. If our lives do not conform to our idea of what is good, we hate our lives. We only love that which we think is good. We think we do not have the fullness of the Christian life because we are not completely healed or in a constant state of euphoria. We even sometimes doubt our faith, and that cannot be good. Based on our idea of what is good, we believe that we are somehow missing the fullness of the Christian life. So we change churches or try to find someone who promises us more than what we presently have. We want a new formula for prayer, worship, or whatever will increase the missing blessings in our lives. But do we know what true blessings are? Or is our idea of a blessing based on our very inadequate and all-too-human idea of what is good? Like Job's comforters, we interpret the circumstances of our lives based on a very inadequate idea of what is good.

What God loves and sees as good is his creation. In the first chapter of Genesis, God repeatedly says of his creation that it was good (see Genesis 1:4, 10, 12, 18, 21, 25). But of all of God's creation, according to Scripture, the greatest good—and what God loves above all else—is to create the likeness of his Son within sinful human beings. Since what God loves and has a passion for is creation—especially the creation that produces the likeness of his son—God's idea of what is good or evil is very different from our own. We deem something good if it satisfies our desire for pleasure or aids us in realizing some end or goal we set for ourselves. The same is true of God, but since the end he has set for himself, and what pleases him above all else, is to reproduce the likeness of his Son, what God sees as good within human beings is their willingness to aid God in accomplishing that end. By contrast, what is not good in human beings is their resistance to that transformation into the likeness of Jesus.

We see this quite clearly in the gospels. Jesus shuns the people who are known as "good people" but instead likes sinners or people who, by our standards, are not good people. Jesus obviously has a different standard. Indeed, it is not a human standard at all, but a divine standard that views evil as resistance to God's purposes and good as cooperation with that purpose. Since God's purpose is to effect radical transformation in our lives, those people who resist are not good in God's sight. Such people are good in their own sight, and for that very reason they resist the transformation God wants to bring about within them. They see no reason for radical transformation. They don't have *eyes that see* or *ears that hear.* By contrast, the sinner often sees the need for radical transformation. The sinner's desperate situation often produces the kind of willingness and surrender God is looking for to accomplish his purpose.

The insight that Jesus has, and we generally lack, is that good people, or people who by human standards are good, have no pressing need to change and allow God to continue his creation within them. The Pharisees of Jesus' day were what we would call good people. But with that goodness came a pride and contentment that prevented the fullness of creation that God wished to bring about within them. Their goodness brought an end to God's creative work in their lives.

For God to continue his creation within us, we can never lose sight of how short we fall of the ultimate good God has for us and our continual need to stay in the process of transformation. As we have seen, to stay in that process of transformation, we need to live in an almost constant state of repentance in order to be open to God's grace and the creation he wishes to continue in our lives. Consequently, our ultimate sin is that we separate ourselves from God and his purpose for our lives. God's purpose is that his creation would continue in our lives and we would be made into the likeness of his Son. Our separation from that purpose is what keeps us from the abundant good God has for us, and it is this separation from which all manner of evil follows. Our real sin is our resistance to the great transformation God wants to bring about within us. Our sin is that we want so much less than what God has for us, and we insist that our pitiful idea of what is good is better than what God has for us.

If this is the nature of sin, then righteousness, at its root, is not a matter of right moral behavior but a continual openness to the transformation God desires to achieve within us. Our openness is founded on a state of repentance that causes us to turn back toward God every time we find ourselves out of his presence because something other than God has captured our attention and affection.

Having now rethought our concepts of sin, evil, and good in the light of the gospel rather than the light that our culture provides, how are we to understand the biblical concept of law? God's law must be rethought, not only because of our renewed understanding of sin, evil, and good, but because the gospel gives us a perspective of law that is radically different from the concept that we acquire as we are acculturated into human society.

Questions for Reflection

1. What is the difference between sin and evil?
2. Can we know what is good or evil?
3. How important is moral order, and how does it relate to God's message?

6

Law and Our
Phenomenal Reality

Our initial understanding of law, like so many of our concepts, is not God-given but is largely the product of human rather than divine agents. We may refer to Moses as the lawgiver, but our idea of law is dervied not from Moses but rather from our parents and society.

Our acquisition of language gives us words, and then we gradually are taught what those words mean through examples or instances to which those words refer. Through this process, the concepts that eventually create our understanding are formed. Our concept of law was not a difficult concept to form because we were supplied with many instances by our parents who, for the sake of order, established laws to govern our behavior. If we broke their laws, we were punished for our disobedience and our disruption of the order they attempted to impose. Even if we were not punished in a traditional sense, we knew of their disapproval by the way their affection for us changed. As we grew older, we experienced the civil law that governs the world beyond our home and family. It, too, was established for the sake of order, and violations of it resulted in disapproval and punishment. There were even police and judges whose only job was to enforce this law and punish violators. When we went to school, we learned that there were physical laws that governed the universe, according to the testimony of esteemed scientists such as Isaac Newton. Violators of this law, it seemed, were punished by nature itself. Thus, it was easy for us to develop the idea that all laws were created for the sake of order, and punishment was the consequence for disobedience.

Thus no wonder we imagine that God, too, must have a law that he wishes to impose upon us. In fact, God's law must be the greatest of laws and therefore must have the greatest of punishments attached to it. We read the Bible and, sure enough, we find a Law (Torah) and we suppose that it, too, must be for the sake of order and obedience.

Jesus, however, tells us that God is a loving Father who awaits the prodigal's return with open arms (see Luke 15:11–32). He tells us that God is preparing a banquet to which all are invited, and the only ones who do not attend are those who imagine that they have better places to be (see Matthew 22:1–14). According to Jesus, the sovereign of the universe is not a lawgiver to whose dictates we must conform or suffer the consequences, but the lawgiver is a loving and approachable father.

The Nature of God's Law

In the gospels, Jesus presents God and the law in a new light, offering a corrective to misunderstandings and applications of the first covenant and law (that is, the Old Testament law given to Moses). If we come to understand, as Jesus had, that we are God's beloved daughters and sons, and God is "*our* Father," then we should also come to understand that God's laws are not about crime and punishment. We should learn from Jesus that the law is not for the sake of order (such as we find in human law), but rather God's laws are intended to guide and direct us into a transformative journey whereby we are made evermore into the likeness of Jesus. With the understanding that Jesus offers, God's law is different from that of our parents, the police, and Isaac Newton. It is not given to meet a need for order within God. Nor is God's law some moral standard that God insists on or is offended when it is violated. God's law does involve morality, but it is not primarily about morality. The intention of the law is to aid human beings in their quest for a right relationship with God and the transformation that comes out of that relationship. God's law is meant as a blessing that guides us into the fullness of life.

Although this interpretation of the law may seem new to contemporary readers, it is actually as ancient as the Church itself. The early Church fathers (particularly those from the East) popularized the theology of "divinization," whereby all were called to be sharers in the divine nature (see 2 Peter 1:4).[1] In contrast, the traditions that we inherited from the Western fathers emphasized the moral life and the reformation of conduct. Unfortunately, our theological interpretation of God's law is sometimes skewed by our obsession with morality. Of course, morality is certainly important, but Jesus is always trying to get at the root of our sin and not merely its outward manifestation. What is at the root of our sin is a wrong relationship with God. With a right relationship with God, morality naturally follows, but moral behavior will never bring us into a right relationship with God. What Jesus teaches, therefore, is not how to be moral but how to have a right relationship with God. The law of Jesus is more blessing than burden.

If law is understood as a blessing that is set forth by a loving father to guide us toward him and away from destruction, we get a very different picture of God. If we understand that God's intention is always to bless us, we can understand God's moral law as a set of promises. That is, God promises that if we walk in his presence, we will not murder, steal, commit adultery, or covet.

Throughout history there have always been some who have come to know God intimately enough that they could understand law in such a light. For most, however, law is not such a divine concept but a very human one of crime and punishment. With such an overly human concept of law, we can tend to form religions founded upon moral righteousness rather than forgiveness. With such a human concept of law, we are led to believe that God rewards the righteous and punishes those who fail to live by God's moral standards. If we believe in a system of divine reward and punishment, and that God's presence is earned solely through moral behavior, then several things follow: either we will never look very deeply into our own hearts for fear of what we might find, or if we do look into our own souls, what we find will convince us that we cannot approach a god who requires perfect moral righteousness. The latter have trouble coming to God because of their awareness of the evil in their hearts, and those who never look into their own hearts develop a religion based on outward behavior and ritual. Those who opt for a behavioral religion never know the reality of their sinfulness and consequently never come to know the greatness of God's mercy.

By contrast, if we found our faith on forgiveness, we are not afraid to look within ourselves and see that, at our core, we are sinners prone to wander from the God who loves us. With knowledge of the sin that lies at our core, we can have compassion for other sinners like ourselves, and we can know the mercy of God beyond our wildest expectations. This is the intimate knowledge God has for us, but it is reserved for the sinner who realizes that entry into God's presence is a matter of God's forgiveness and mercy, and not our righteousness.

Additionally, it is only such a sinner who can rejoice when Jesus tells us that *"it is easier for heaven and earth to pass away, than for one stroke of a letter in the law to be dropped"* (Luke 16:17). Only the sinner who has experienced God's forgiveness and mercy knows that the law is not the threat of a wrathful God, but the promise of a loving Father. Unfortunately, most of us do not have such an understanding; instead we understand law as did the Pharisees—as a set of commands to which we must conform or suffer the consequences.

Our human experience has certainly prepared us to understand God's law in such a negative way, but another reason often influences our preference for such a wrong understanding. This view allows us to convince ourselves and others that we really are good. We seek to be better than others and therefore need a law of reward and punishment to establish our moral superiority and goodness. But there is only one who is good, and it is only through his forgiveness and mercy that we come to dwell in his presence.

Fortunately, in spite of this fact that we misunderstand the nature of law, our misunderstanding is not necessarily all bad. Human misunderstanding can serve as a starting point for our relationship with God. Personal relationships always begin in misunderstanding, and our all-too-human understanding of law can provide the kind of initial misunderstanding we need to begin our relationship with God. If we are to be changed and made into God's likeness, we must begin somewhere or with some understanding, or misunderstanding, of who we are and who God is. A human concept of law is capable of providing such an understanding from which we might begin this transformative process.

As children, our first sense of identity comes from law, particularly from our parents and their social network (other children, friends, extended family, and so forth). We have an innate need for boundaries that teach us how to interact with the world (physically and socially) and they protect us from harm. The law, which our parents and others imposed, contributed greatly to our first sense of identity. Contemporary psychology tells us that children initially conceive rules or laws to be absolute and inflexible. Thus, a strict notion of law may be a necessary starting point for the human psyche. However, as necessary as this starting point may be, the maturation process involves our realization that not all rules are "hard-and-fast" rules. Not all laws are like those that govern mathematics. Some rules—what I call "soft" rules—help us to structure paragraphs effectively or guide us to strike a ball properly when playing a sport. Soft rules provide direction. For example, one does not have to swing a bat according to the rules of baseball or cricket, but the ball is sure to fly farther if we follow the practiced norm. Similarly, we are not required to follow every rule of speech or grammar, but doing so helps others understand what we wish to communicate.

As we mature we learn the limits and application of soft and hard rules. Far from limiting our potential, we gradually discern how soft rules allow us to maximize our mental, spiritual, and physical potential. This maturation process can help us understand God and our relationship with him. For many of us, since we spend little time developing a relationship with God, we retain our childish understanding of God and imagine that all of God's rules are hard rules for the sake of order and obedience. We imagine that God, like our parents or our society, wants to maintain order and therefore, imposes rigid laws. But God is certainly not preoccupied with order and control, as should be obvious from the chaotic state of the world. Unlike most parents or our human legal system or even some scientific views of the universe, God's ultimate purpose is not to establish order and force conformity to his every dictate. God is not a control freak like us, but such is the initial concept for most of us, particularly since our original conception of God is little more than a projection of ourselves. Such a misconception, however, is not a bad place from which to begin. It seems that identity, either for individuals or groups of people, in its early stages of development, requires fixed and rigid boundaries.

Upon coming out of Egypt, for example, the Jewish people had little sense of identity because of their enslavement and assimilation into Egyptian society. In order to establish some sense of identity, they had to establish cultural and religious norms. Such norms require boundaries. The law provided just such boundaries from which norms and a cultural identity might be formed. The law that God gave to Moses was not primarily a set of moral rules for the sake of order. Certainly there was a moral element, but the law was not primarily about morality. It included all sorts of social practices, such as dietary laws, laws concerning property rights, religious festivals, animal sacrifices, vestments for priests, finance, and a host of other sundry laws. In other words, God loved them and provided them with the kind of rules that a people would need to establish a cultural identity.

Of course, it is hard to see the law as such a blessing if we never get beyond our human view of order and punishment. In fact, to understand God's law as a blessing, we need to understand God as the loving Father that Jesus reveals. Since few of us are willing to persist long enough to receive that perspective, and most of us are obsessed with averting crime and punishment, we read morality into every aspect of God's law. We imagine that breaking the law angers God, just as our breaking of human law angers our neighbors.

Jesus undermines this naive understanding of the law. He does not, however, undermine the law and customs of the Jews—for such laws will always be a blessing from God that give the Jewish people an identity and a place from which to dialogue with God. Rather, Jesus challenges the misinterpretation of the law as the ultimate end or goal for humanity. We are not servants of the law; we are servants of God and one another. When the Pharisees question Jesus about breaking the law concerning the Sabbath, he tells them that *"the sabbath was made for humankind, and not humankind for the sabbath"* (Mark 2:27). This is true not simply concerning the law of the Sabbath but the law in general. The law has no objective value in itself. The law is an instrument and not an end. It is meant to provide a place from which a personal, communal, and intimate relationship with God might begin.

The law provides a starting point for our relationship with God by providing us with a sense that we are good for having kept its precepts—even though "being good" is not a prerequisite for the relationship. Many of us need to begin our relationships with a sense that we are good because we fear that we will not be loved if we do not conform to the law that our parents, society, and God set forth before us. Without such a belief in our own goodness, many of us could never believe that anyone, and most especially God, could love us. Our self-imposed obsession with our goodness is usually the starting point for our relationship with God.

Since we begin with the understanding that God is like us and only loves that which is good, many of us need to begin with a sense that we are somehow good in God's sight. Keeping the law can certainly give us that sense. Eventually, however, if we enter and stay in relationship with God, we will see that God's love for us is not due to our goodness, but to the greatness of God's love. Thus, it matters little where we begin our relationship with God, but only that we *do* begin. If we enter and stay in relationship with him, God will eventually reveal to us who we truly are, with all of our sin and waywardness. Through this process, God reveals himself as a father whose love for us is greater than we can think or imagine—greater than our sinfulness, weakness, and our limited human capacity to love.

Jesus understood that God was his loving father, and that nothing could separate him from his Father's love. It is only when we take on Jesus' perspective, and see ourselves as beloved daughters and sons of God, that we are able to properly understand the things that God wishes to communicate to us. If we do not understand God as our loving father, as Jesus did, we will always distort what God is trying to communicate to us.

The Bible provides a record of God speaking in various ways that accommodate our distorted understanding. Merold Westphal, in his book *Overcoming Onto-Theology*, quotes a professor of his as having said that "the Bible is the Divinely revealed misinformation about God."[2] According to Westphal, our reception of God's word can be compared to a three-year-old who puts a coin in his mouth. Parents who force the child to spit out the coin can expect the question, "Why?" Most children are not going to understand viruses and bacteria, so parents may explain that there are "invisible bugs on them that can make you sick if they get inside you."[3] In a sense, we can be like naive children when it comes to understanding God's authentic voice. Fortunately, through the Bible, God speaks to people who can only grasp the truth relative to their conceptual understanding.

Very often when I press God for more insight or revelation, I sense his response: "Jim, if I explained it to you, you wouldn't understand." Since God's communication to us is always framed by the limits of our understanding, it is difficult for God to communicate otherwise. God can only communicate what we can understand. Or, put another way, we can only record God's voice in a way that makes sense to us. If we follow the Old Testament carefully, we can see how God was able to communicate with greater and greater clarity, but it is not until Jesus that we receive the ultimate understanding of God as our loving father. This is the perspective or understanding that we all need to reach to correctly understand what God is trying to communicate to us. Of course, we tend not to begin there. Rather, we begin with our *mis*understanding. The many narratives of the Bible—Old Testament and New Testament—account for the various phases of our faith journey, from our misunderstanding of God nature, to the ultimate understanding of God as our loving father.

The Biblical Revelation

The Bible begins with the almost universal misunderstanding that God, like human beings, loves what he loves and hates what he hates. If we happen to do what he hates, he is angered and must be appeased. We imagine that our only hope is to put our sin, or what we believe God hates, on someone or something else. This was the idea of the scapegoat. The scapegoat (see Leviticus 16:8–10) was a ritual by which the people would place their sin upon a goat and then chase the goat into the desert, thereby ridding themselves of their sin and making themselves sinless and pleasing to God. The idea of the scapegoat took other forms as well. Human sacrifice, which was still widely practiced in early biblical times and eventually came to be replaced by animal sacrifice, was also a form of scapegoating. Today the major form of scapegoating is a matter of seeing other people as the cause of one's own sin. If others are seen as the cause of our sin, we appear less sinful and "more good." All of this is based on the widespread assumption that we must be sinless in order to find favor with God.

The Book of Job addresses this misunderstanding of sin and God's response to it. Job's comforters insist that Job must have sinned in order for such evil to befall him. This is very typical of our initial understanding of our relationship with God. That is, good things happen if we do what is pleasing to God, and bad things happen if we do what angers God. Of course, the very explicit point of the Book of Job is to demonstrate the opposite—that God's love for us is not swayed by our sinfulness or good deeds. Nevertheless, the theology of Job's comforters appears throughout the Old Testament and continues to impact society today.

Some Old Testament narratives attest to our inaccurate human perception of God; but still, we never seem to get it. Some have said that kings have a divine right to rule, but the Bible says it was the will of human beings and not God that created kings among the ancient Hebrews (see 1 Samuel 8:4–9). The Pharisees claimed that Moses spoke God's will, but Jesus tells us that the law was given because of the hardness of human hearts and not because of God's will (see Matthew 19:8). Human beings are constantly misinterpreting God's communication and then claiming that their misinterpretation is God's intentional meaning. The Bible chronicles all sorts of people, at all sorts of places in their process of coming to know God, and it is not always easy to discern the difference between a mature understanding and a primitive understanding of God. This makes some people wonder how (or if) the Scriptures were inspired by God.

What does it mean to be the inspired word of God? For a long time *inspiration* was taken to mean that the words of Scripture revealed an objective portrait of God—sort of like Newton's laws of physics. The same was thought about reality in general. Many still believe that humans are able to perceive the actual and objective reality of the world. Much has occurred over the last two centuries to change that view. From our current, postmodern perspective, we realize that we can only have a phenomenal understanding of the world (that is, knowledge filtered through our human concepts). The same is true concerning our understanding of God.

Given this fact, much of Scripture must be understood from the perspective of our inadequate human experience. In order to overcome the disparity between the transcendence of God and human life, God became human. Thus Jesus provides a perspective that is both human and more than human—a perspective like no other. Jesus, in being both divine and human, provides not just a revelation of God, but the ultimate revelation of how human beings should understand God. God gives us *eyes that see and ears that hear.*

By understanding the uniqueness of the revelation that Jesus offers, we also attain a better understanding of how the narratives of Scripture unfold the many stages of our faith journey. Jesus tells us in the Sermon on the Mount that the ancient understanding of God's ultimate standard was actually just the first step toward knowing God. We can return to the example of murder [or killing] that we used in chapter 4:

> *"You have heard that it was said to those of ancient times, 'You shall not murder' [or 'kill' in some translations]; and 'whoever murders shall be liable to judgment.' But I say to you that if you are angry with a brother or sister, you will be liable to judgment"* (Matthew 5:21–22).

In verses 27, 33, 43 of the same chapter of Matthew, Jesus repeats the phrase, *you have heard that it was said*, after which he brings further understanding to the command. In other words, he wants us to compare his wording with the words of his predecessors and realize the incompleteness of the old law. Notice that I said *incomplete,* not *incorrect.* God's original covenant always remains, but Jesus clarifies its meaning to enhance our understanding of God. In some cases, Jesus appears to outright contradict the Hebrew law—*"Love your enemies,"* he says, *"so that you may be children of your Father in heaven"* (Matthew 5:44–45). In contrast, the ancients thought it was permissible to hate their enemies. In fact, their interpretation of God seemed to indicate the need to hate their enemies. Now Jesus teaches them to arm themselves with love.

Some have traditionally interpreted the idea of loving one's enemies in the narrow sense of love for one's own tribe or private community. As such, it is possible to accept Jesus' command to love our enemies without contradicting the Old Testament accounts of killing other tribes and nations. This narrow understanding of Jesus' command allows us to reconcile the Old Testament prescription for killing enemies with Jesus' prescription to love enemies. Such an interpretation, however, keeps us from coming into the fullness of the gospel and being made evermore into God's likeness. Indeed, Jesus tells us in the very next line that the reason we are to love our enemies is so that we might be like God himself (see Matthew 5:45), one who loves both the righteous and unrighteous and blesses those who are evil as well as those who are good. Luke's

Gospel tells us that *"he is kind to the ungrateful and the wicked"* (Luke 6:35).

Obviously, God loves all of his creation and tells us to do the same. Furthermore, Jesus' message is not a contradiction to what was set forth in the Old Testament, as long as we understand that the revelation that Jesus offers provides a better perspective from which to understand God.

In a sense, Jesus' message shares the warning of postmodernism. That is, Jesus asks us to strip away our presuppositions, not only with respect to the Old Testament, but with respect to our own cultural baggage. Christians today can no longer pretend that the Scripture affords an objective view of God. The fullness of the gospel has been suppressed due to our misunderstanding of Scripture as the ultimate, final, knowable, objective account of God. Our self-professed understanding of God makes it very easy for us to dismiss the challenging words of Jesus in favor of the more human perspective of God that appears throughout Scripture and which instructs us in ways contrary to what Jesus commands. We are too easily convinced that Jesus did not mean what he said. He cannot really mean that we are to love our enemies (see Matthew 5:44), since God told the people of old to kill their enemies. Jesus must not really mean that we are not to swear any oaths (see Matthew 5:34), since elsewhere we were instructed to keep our oaths. Jesus cannot really mean that we are not to store up treasure on earth (see Matthew 6:19–21), since the God of old had blessed those whom he favored with earthly treasure.

At this point many might interject, "But what about judgment? Even Jesus spoke of judgment" (see Matthew 25:31–46), but his version of judgment is not what we expected. According to Jesus, we have all failed to do to *"the least of these"* (Matthew 25:40) as we would do unto the Lord, and we do not live according to the Sermon on the Mount or even the Ten Commandments. Jesus' words should warn us that we are in need of forgiveness and mercy. No one comes to God through their obedience or goodness. We all come to God by God's goodness, not by what we do or do not do.

God's Judgment

Throughout the Old and New Testaments we discover the many ways that we have failed to be in a right relationship with God. We also learn how (because of the suffering and death of Jesus) and why (because of forgiveness and love) God offers redemption for our failures. Redemption involves two interrelated elements. First, it involves the judgment that we are guilty and have failed to be in a right relationship with God, but second, it also involves God's willingness to pay for our failure and the destructive evil that follows from our not being in a right relationship with God. This second element of redemption is beautifully revealed through Jesus' suffering and death on the cross, but it must be preceded by judgment. Forgiveness and judgment are integrally related because without the judgment that one is guilty, there is no need for forgiveness or mercy. Of course, it is possible for someone to reject forgiveness or mercy because they insist that they are innocent, but such self-appraisals are not usually based on God's judgment. So separation from God is possible, but it is not the result of any lack of forgiveness or mercy on God's part. Since God's desire for relationship is so much greater than our own, it is difficult for us to see the extent of God's forgiveness—indeed, God heals our sin in ways that we cannot comprehend.

For example, it is not that the prodigal son did no evil. His guilt is not dissipated, but the father's forgiveness is greater than the prodigal's evil. The prodigal son could have chosen to remain with the pigs (see Luke 15:11–32), just as we can choose to reject God's forgiveness and mercy in our lives. If the prodigal chose to reject his father, we would very likely reason that he got what he deserved, and it was God's judgment upon his wicked ways. Such a hellish existence would not have been the result of God's will, but the choice of the prodigal son. Jesus tells us that God is the loving father of the prodigal (representing us) who requires nothing more than that he return to his Father (representing God). In fact, God is so unconventional that even the conditions of our return do not matter. The prodigal son, for example, was not overcome with love and affection for his father; rather, he ran to his father in hunger to avert eating with pigs. Regardless of the reason, the father *"ran and put his arms around him and kissed him"* (Luke 15:20).

But what of all the talk in Scripture of God's wrath? How does that square with the God whom Jesus reveals in the gospels? Many explanations have been offered. In the early Church some argued that the god of the Old Testament was a different god than the God that Jesus reveals in the New Testament. Others have maintained that they are merely different aspects of the same God: Jesus manifests one aspect of God, while the wrath of God seen in the Old Testament is another aspect of God. Still others maintain that the great difference between the Old Testament God and the God of the gospels reveals the inconsistency of Scripture and is evidence that the Scripture is not inspired. Since we now know that human reality is a phenomenal reality, or reality as perceived by human beings, we are in a position to understand the Scripture as God's revelation of who human beings perceive God to be.

Phenomenal Revelation

When we thought that we lived in an objective reality, largely untainted by our own perspective, it was natural to suppose that the biblical revelation was equally a revelation of objective reality, or the reality of God's objective identity. Since we now know that the nature of the reality into which God has placed us is a phenomenal reality and objectivity is beyond us, it should be obvious that the nature of God's revelation is also phenomenal.

As a phenomenal revelation of who we understand God to be—rather than some impossible notion of God's objective identity—the Bible contains a variety of narratives that reflect many phases of our dynamic relationship with God. For example, we can find narratives that portray our initial, ill-conceived notion of God. As explored previously, God is sometimes portrayed as some ultimate authority intent upon law and order. It is no wonder that this is where we begin in our understanding of God, since a god of wrath, intent upon law and order, mirrors our experience with human authority. Therefore, it should also not be surprising that our ancestors recorded this interpretation of God as part of their communication with God. This is not to say that Scripture is the product of human beings expressing who they imagine God to be. It is rather God's revelation of how humans imagine God to be, and how God continues to work in their lives to reveal a God very different from who they had imagined. Just as we grow in our understanding of the law, so, too, the narratives of Scripture unfold and reveal the maturing of the relationship between God and humanity. This process of maturation—of coming to know how God truly forgives and saves us—is known as the history of salvation (or salvation history, *Heilsgeschichte*). This variety of revelation reflects what we experience in our individual lives. The overall impact of Scripture also provides a beautiful picture of how we are to be like our heavenly Father and patiently minister to people who have ill-conceived notions of God and self.

The fact that we progress through stages to discover God's (and our own) true identity should not be taken to mean that the Jews of the Old Testament had a lesser relationship with God than New Testament (or contemporary) Christians. The people of the Old Testament had a rich understanding of God, with an acute awareness of God's mercy in a way that many Christians today do not.

Very few of us can accept the full impact of Jesus' message and, therefore, the Bible depicts human beings at all sorts of places in their journey toward that ultimate revelation. Our faith journey, like that of the Bible, often involves falling and rising up—sin and forgiveness. Of course, God loves us even when we fall. God loves us even with our ill-conceived notions of his identity. We all begin with a wrong understanding, but God loves us just as much at the early stages of our relationship with him as at the latter stages. The fullness of life, as we experience it, only comes with the Jesus revelation that God is our father and nothing can separate us from his love. Without that understanding, human life will always be less than what God intends for us.

Although God loves us, both as individuals and as a species, despite our misunderstanding of him, fullness of life only comes by understanding how to love like God—which means we must know God and ourselves without our cultural, human bias. The understanding of God as "Father," as taught by Jesus, allows us to know the fullness of life that God has for us. It allows us to dwell in the ultimate, phenomenal reality of God's blessings. To know this ultimate reality, we need to live in an awareness of the fact that nothing can separate us from his love.

This chapter has shown that the concept of law, as acquired by us through our experience with human society, is different from our concept of law from the perspective of Jesus. Thus, the biblical revelation accounts for our phenomenal understanding of God. Revelation culminates in the perspective that God is our father and nothing can separate us from his love. Given this better understanding of both God's law and revelation, we are now in a better position to understand the very heart of the gospel, particularly the concepts of atonement and forgiveness.

Questions for Reflection

1. What is the difference among civil, religious, scientific, and personal laws?
2. How does contemporary culture help or hinder our understanding of God's law?
3. Compare and contrast Jesus' law with Moses' law.

7

Atonement, Forgiveness, and Perspectivalism

The belief that Jesus died for our sins is a belief that unites Christians, but what does it mean? How did his death reconcile, *atone,* or "make us one" with God? Much disagreement has existed concerning the specific nature of the atonement. What *is* agreed on is the fact that Jesus' death was reparation for human sin, and that through his death the relationship between human beings and God is restored. Jesus himself says that he came *"to give his life a ransom for man"* (Matthew 20:28 and Mark 10:45). If the atonement involves a ransom or payment, which the Scripture seems so clear about, who receives the payment, and what does it assure? These questions are not clearly answered in Scripture, and so there have been a variety of theories concerning atonement and the nature of the payment.

As we have already learned, we must be very careful when we use human concepts to describe God. This is particularly true with respect to the atonement. We may never be able to take in the fullness of what happened on the cross. Still, we need to fashion an understanding for ourselves that is both consistent with what is revealed in the gospels and best enables us to follow Jesus into the fullness of life he has for us. It is from such a perspective that we proceed.

The Historical Views

The view of atonement that dominated the early and medieval Church is referred to as *Christus Victor* (Christ the Victor) and can be traced to several of the early Church fathers, particularly Origen (185–254) and Gregory of Nyssa (335–394). Their theology proclaimed the victory over Satan, with the implication that God, through the cross of Christ, out-witted the deceiver (Satan). The sacrifice of Christ on the cross is known as *penal substitution* (also known as sacrificial expiation), that is, the sacrifice of one life for another. According to Athanasius (296–373), if we do not heed God's warning to Adam, then our sin, too, must be rectified by the death penalty (see Genesis 2:17). The atonement, then, is Jesus substituting his life for ours to repay our debt. Many took this to mean that Satan was responsible for the murder of Jesus and, there-fore, that our debt was paid to Satan in exchange for our freedom. Ac-cording to this view, humanity was forced into sin by Satan, and thus God was forced to fight back. However, Anselm of Canterbury (1033–1109) and his infamous *Cur Deus Homo* emphasized that God did not intervene with violence to gain victory over the enemy.

> God would have been doing unjust violence against the devil, since the latter was the lawful possessor of man; for the devil had not gained his hold over man with violence; rather it was man who had gone over to the devil of his own free will.[1]

Anselm was adamant that ransom was *not* paid to Satan because Satan had no legal claim over human beings in the first place. Neither Satan nor human beings belong to anyone but God; nor does either stand outside God's power.[2] According to Anselm's theory (often re-ferred to as the satisfaction theory), God's honor was offended by sin, and Jesus' death was necessary to satisfy God's offended honor. Thus, the payment is to God and not the devil. A variation of this view was held by Thomas Aquinas (1225–1274) and the sixteenth-century re-formers, particularly Martin Luther and John Calvin (1509–1564). They maintained that divine law required punishment for sin and that Jesus suffered in humanity's place.[3]

Another interpretation of the atonement is known as the moral influence theory. It was originally advanced by Peter Abelard (1079–1142). Abelard agreed with Anselm in rejecting the idea of a payment to Satan, but thought that Anselm's satisfaction theory portrayed God as vengeful.[4] As an alternative view, Abelard claimed that it was neither Satan who required the death of Jesus (ransom motif) nor God (satisfaction motif), but human beings, insofar as human beings needed to see the extent of God's love for them. "The divine love which is exhibited in the death of Christ provokes a response of love in the sinner which overcomes his contempt of God."[5]

Although a host of theories appeared throughout the medieval period, most were variations on these three major theories, with the satisfaction theory becoming the most popular. Since both Thomas Aquinas and the reformers endorsed the satisfaction theory, it became the view of both mainstream Protestantism and Catholicism. Over the past two centuries, however, there has been opposition to that dominant view.

The revivalists of the nineteenth century were "embarrassed by the Calvinistic doctrine of penal substitution,"[6] which leaves us with a god whose honor is greater than his love for his son—a god who must be appeased even at the cost of his son's life. This view also gives us a picture of an exacting god who really does not love us, but must be bought off. Such a theory is especially absurd when we consider the images presented in the movie, *The Passion of the Christ*. The satisfaction theory would have us believe that the enormous suffering Jesus endured was at the hand of his own Father who sought to have his honor vindicated. Furthermore, that wrath that Jesus endured was meant for you and me. With such an image of God we may be able to obey him, or even serve him, but who could ever fall in love with such a god?

Consequently, some theologians rejected the idea that the atonement was a matter of God's wrath.[7] Paul Peter Waldenstrom (1838–1917), for instance, held the view that the fall of humanity took place only in us and "the fall of man did not cause any change in the heart of God."[8] Recall that sin is a matter of human beings turning away from God, but sin does not cause God to turn away from human beings. Therefore, there is no need for restoration on God's part. In fact, "the atonement reveals God's presence with us in our sinfulness."[9] Unlike the satisfaction theory, these more contemporary notions of atonement make God much more approachable, but where in such theories is the payment that Scripture seems so clear about?

Atonement as Forgiveness

Another possibility is that the payment that is mentioned in Scripture, instead of being a payment to God, Satan, or even human beings, is the payment that forgiveness requires. With forgiveness there is certainly a payment, although it is not necessarily a payment to any specific person (or deity). When one person does harm to another, the relationship between them is damaged or destroyed. Someone must pay for the harm that has been done. There is, however, an option concerning who will pay for the offense. It could be, as in the case of civil justice, that the guilty pay for the harm they have done to the innocent. In some cases, justice may bring restoration to a relationship. In most cases it does not, and justice merely brings closure and not restoration. The other option is for the innocent, who has suffered the harm, to be willing to absorb that hurt and not demand retribution. The harm the innocent willingly suffers is able to restore the relationship insofar as harm terminates with the innocent's willingness to suffer the offense. Thus the victim "pays" for the harm that has been done, and the relationship is restored between the innocent and the offender. A payment is made, but it is not made to a specific person.

Imagine someone taking a friend's credit card without permission and using it to go on a great vacation. In realizing that the thousands of dollars they had charged to the friend's account has hurt their friend and damaged the relationship, they experience regret and wish to restore the relationship. Of course, this requires restoration for the harm they have done. In order to restore the relationship, the offense must be "paid for." One way to pay for the offense and thus restore the relationship is through justice, whereby the guilty party compensates the innocent friend for what has been done. If, however, the guilty party is unable to compensate and pay back the money, the only other possible means of restoring the relationship is through forgiveness. In such a case, the relationship is restored by the innocent party's willingness to forgive the guilty party. In restoring the relationship through forgiveness rather than justice, the innocent must be willing to pay for what has been charged to their account and no longer treat the friend as guilty. Thus, in a sense, forgiveness is also the fulfillment of justice in that with forgiveness the debt is satisfied. This is certainly the case with God. In the case of sin, God makes the payment to himself, which means that he suffers the loss.

In the parable of the unmerciful servant (Matthew 18:23–35), the king who forgave the ten-thousand-talent debt suffered the loss of ten thousand talents because he chose to forgive the debt. He paid the debt, even though there was no exchange of money. Forgiveness always costs something and for that reason, it is so rare. The high cost of forgiveness is the reason that the man who had been forgiven by the king was not willing to forgive the debt of the man who owed him. He obviously thought that the cost of forgiving the debt was greater than his love for the one who asked for his mercy.

Of course, the debt that is to be forgiven is not always monetary, but there is still always a cost. Many times what it costs us to forgive is our appearance of righteousness. When we refuse to forgive, we insist—consciously or subconsciously—that everyone know that we are the innocent victim, and the other party is the guilty one. When we forgive, however, we do not care if the entire world thinks that we are the guilty one as long as the relationship with the guilty party is restored. Jesus hangs on a cross, and he does not care if the entire world thinks that he is a criminal. With forgiveness the innocent is willing to assume the guilt and pay the price for the sake of love. Thus, this kind of love and forgiveness, which is the only means of restoring relationships that have been seriously damaged, always requires the death of the false self or who we think we are and the image we wish to portray. We are usually not able to suffer the cost of our reputation.

Consider the example of adultery. The one who is hurt is innocent, but if that person truly forgives, the innocent person says that she or he is willing to endure pain without requiring retribution or some type of payment on the part of the guilty person. The innocent one who has been offended accepts the hurt and treats the guilty as if no wrong has been done. The relationship is restored, and the guilty one is able to enjoy that relationship as if nothing ever happened. Something, however, certainly did happen, but the innocent person is willing to pay for the offense for the sake of restoring the relationship. In fact, the relationship may be better than ever, at least to the extent that the guilty party realizes that the innocent one cherishes the relationship to the extent of being willing to pay dearly to preserve it.

The situation is quite different for the innocent who forgives. The innocent person must calculate whether the desire to restore the relationship to its previous state is worth the enormous pain that must be endured to do so. When most of us make such a calculation, we are only willing to forgive if we judge the hurt to be something we can bear. If we think the offense is unbearable, we choose not to restore the relationship, and by so doing we equally choose not to forgive; that is, we do not forgive as God forgives.

I remember a story about a woman who had been raped and her entire family killed by a gang of soldiers. Years later, while working as a nurse, a soldier was brought to her hospital on the brink of death. The nurse recognized him as the officer in charge of the men who raped her and killed her family. After eight days the man had been nursed back to health by this woman, and, upon regaining consciousness, he was told that the only reason he was brought back from the brink of death was because of the loving care of this woman. Upon recognizing her, he was taken back, and asked why she would do such a thing. She replied by telling him that she followed one who said *"love your enemies"* (Matthew 5:44).

Regardless of how grand her act of forgiveness may seem to us, it does not approach the forgiveness of God. In fact, there is no adequate human version of forgiveness that equals the sacrifice of the cross. With respect to the nurse and the rapist, the closest comparison to Christ's sacrifice would be the outrageous suggestion that the nurse be willing to marry the soldier to emulate Christ's intimate love for the worst evildoers. It is difficult for us to imagine a scenario in which a rape victim is willing to marry her abuser. Such a union would require death to all fear. It would require death to our identity, perhaps at the expense of our reputation and dignity. Such a death would certainly be painful. Forgiveness—real forgiveness that restores relationships—always involves a painful death. Such an act of forgiveness and love, along with the pain and death that come with it, is exactly what Jesus so beautifully manifests on the cross.

Most of us do not consider ourselves great sinners who require great forgiveness. We have never murdered or raped and, therefore, God would not have to suffer to forgive and enter into an intimate relationship with us in the way that the nurse would have to suffer to enter into an intimate relationship with the soldier. But we all have murdered, at least in our hearts. As we saw in the Sermon on the Mount, Jesus tells us that those who hate are guilty of murder (see Matthew 5:21–22). Equating hate with murder may seem unrealistic. We may imagine that thoughts of hatred are harmless and only the act itself brings destruction. But what if we were aware of other's thoughts—their rejection, malice, spite, and so forth? What if we were omniscient and knew of every unkind thought our spouses or friends ever had toward us? What if we knew of every time our spouses preferred the company of someone else? If we were such creatures, our limited capacity for forgiveness would leave us with no long-lasting relationships. God, however, is just such an omniscient being. He knows our every wayward thought.

Furthermore, as we have seen in previous chapters, the pain and suffering that God experiences is not merely the result of our heart's rejection of him. It also results from the fact that God knows that the life he has for us is so much greater than the life we choose for ourselves. We are his beloved children, and he suffers when we resist his presence and the fullness of life he has for us. God's pain and suffering is like that of a parent who knows of their children's dreadful destination. God's response to that pain is forgiveness. That is, he suffers the pain for the sake of restoration.

The father of the prodigal son has lost half of his estate because of his young son's sin, but he gained back his son, and that is all that mattered. His older son, however, valued the estate more than the brother and thus could not comprehend the father's reconciliation. Therein lies the difference between God and human beings. We tend to be like the older son, who thinks that the loss of his tangible estate is greater than something as intangible as love. Of course, the call of the Christian life is that we would follow Jesus and therein begin to love like the father of the prodigal son.

Much of what it means to follow Jesus is very appealing. We want to have a relationship with the Father as he had. We want the power of the Holy Spirit to flow through us as it flowed through him. However, it is not appealing to suffer injustice for the sake of restoring relationship with the guilty. There is something very unappealing about the innocent paying for the offenses of the guilty. It certainly seems unfair that the guilty are free from the consequences of what they have done and can enjoy the relationship with the innocent as if the offense never took place, while the innocent must suffer the pain of the offense.

No one likes to suffer, but the fact that suffering is the result of injustice makes it especially difficult to bear. The reason we find injustice so hard to accept, however, follows from the fact that we generally conceive of ourselves as innocent. We readily imagine the injustice being done to us, but have trouble seeing ourselves as the guilty party. If we were able to perceive ourselves as the guilty party, we would not find forgiveness so unappealing. Unfortunately, few of us imagine ourselves as guilty, and thus few of us are willing to suffer much pain in order to love.

This concept of forgiveness provides a way to understand how God can be just, demand payment for an offense, and forgiving in his willingness to be the one who pays for the offense, all at the same time. This idea of atonement as forgiveness also gives us a way to better understand the suffering of Jesus and the nature of the Godhead. One of the problems with the satisfaction theory and the idea that the Father poured out his wrath upon his Son, is that in Christian theology the Father and Son are united within the oneness of a triune Godhead. If God is three persons, yet one, how can we understand the Father's wrath being poured out on Jesus for the sake of satisfying the Father's honor? If the Father and Jesus are one, then by the Father pouring his wrath upon Jesus, he is in fact pouring his wrath upon himself. Since they are one, the punishment leveled upon Jesus is equally leveled upon the Father as well. In a very real sense that is exactly what happens when God decides to forgive human beings for our rejection of the relationship he desires to have with us, and all the destruction that follows. All three persons of the Godhead, and not just Jesus, suffer the offense that Jesus manifests. Thus, by understanding the nature of forgiveness, and by understanding that atonement is essentially a matter of forgiveness, we have a better perspective from which to view the cross and equally the nature of God.

Forgiveness also helps us understand the nature of Jesus' suffering. With the satisfaction theory, it was assumed that Jesus suffers like a human on the cross. Since, according to that theory, he is our substitute and suffers punishment on our behalf, many assumed that it was his humanity that suffered and not his divinity. In fact, some versions of the satisfaction theory would have us imagine that God separates himself from Jesus because a holy God cannot be in the presence of sin, and Jesus has taken our sin upon himself. Thus, Jesus on the cross represents human beings and not God. According to that theory, his suffering represents humanity's fate before God.

The better perspective, however, is that Jesus' suffering is fully human *and* fully divine. That is, Jesus' suffering is not just the suffering of a man but the suffering of God as well.

I Am the Way, the Truth, and the Life

By understanding atonement as largely a matter of forgiveness, we also acquire a much better understanding of what Jesus means when he says *"I am the way, and the truth, and the life. No one comes to the Father except through me"* (John 14:6). Many Christians take this to mean that no one comes to God unless they accept their specific interpretation of Jesus. Those who belong to this special group are saved and all others are excluded. But certainly the Gospel of John cannot be referring to the universal acceptance of a single theology for Jesus. If salvation is truly from God, then we all come to God through the forgiveness that Jesus manifests on the cross and not because we have a particular, correct theology.

Many are disappointed in a God who loves all of his children and does not prefer the good son more than the prodigal. Such "good" people are often indignant at such injustice and would find it hell to endure the eternal presence of a forgiving God. They perceive that goodness must be rewarded, and evil punished. Consequently, they are very disappointed with a God who chooses to suffer evil rather than punish it.

A Contemporary Understanding

Although I believe that atonement is more a matter of forgiveness than ransom, satisfaction, or moral influence, there is still more that we need to understand concerning atonement. The matter is more complicated today than in the past, and thus we need to consider the matter from the perspective of our contemporary, postmodern understanding. The concepts that lie at the base of our understanding are not necessarily God's concepts, but rather concepts relative to human language communities, culture, history, and individual philosophies and experiences. The concepts through which we form our understanding were once believed to be, for the most part, God-given, and therefore the understanding they formed represented objective reality. As we have learned, it is very difficult to defend the notion of "objective truth" in light of what we know about cultural variation, language formation, and an intellectual history that presents us with countless combinations of unique philosophical perspectives. Today we are aware that our concepts are not God's concepts but our own. Even though there is an objective world that we experience, our understanding of that world is shaped by a host of factors that are rooted in human freedom and imagination.

Furthermore, our contemporary, postmodern insight has also brought us to understand that our concepts are not simply defined in and for themselves but acquire their meaning from their relationship to other concepts. Thus, our concept of atonement, whatever it may be, is shaped by a myriad of other concepts, which all have a part in forming our concept of atonement. Our cultural and historical concepts of things such as justice, forgiveness, love, and sin all have their effects on our concept of atonement. Most importantly, our concept of God interacts with and influences all of our other theological concepts. Of course, our concept of God also will be influenced by a host of other factors, such as the identity of our parents, where and with whom we studied, and where we go or don't go to church. It is for these reasons that we see a myriad of perspectives on atonement. Anselm's picture of atonement presupposes a God who is regal and motivated by honor. More contemporary versions of the doctrine are certainly influenced by notions of God as less wrathful and less motivated by honor. It seems obvious that the reason Anselm and Abelard have different understandings of atonement after reading the same Scripture is not because one is more intelligent and better in tune with reason, but that they have different concepts that comprise their understanding. In other words, individuals with different experiences and histories will fashion different concepts that will affect their notion of atonement.

Faced with the reality that our concepts are interconnected and are affected by one another—all of which are affected by cultural, historical, and philosophical perspectives—how are we to achieve a *true* understanding? Many respond to this threat by simply denying the postmodern critique of the nature of our understanding. A better response is to realize that the only reason we are threatened by this situation is because of our misconception of what would constitute a true understanding. Modernity had imagined that a true understanding should be some sort of definitive certainty after the model of mathematics. Christianity, however, is all about knowing a personal God. If we wish to understand the truth of a person, be they human or divine, the kind of abstract and objective thinking that became so popular in the modern period is inappropriate. To know the truth of a person we must dialogue.

In a personal dialogue, when we attempt to make ourselves known to another person, there is a constant revealing of who we are and a constant misunderstanding on the part of the interlocutor. We attempt to correct misunderstandings, but, as any married person knows, sometimes misunderstandings continue and our intentional meaning is always a little out of reach. That does not, however, mean that we do not communicate an understanding of those persons (including God) with whom we are involved in intimate dialogue. Although no one ever achieves a complete understanding of another person, our subjective understanding of one another grows as we remain in open dialogue.

It matters little where dialogue begins, since our initial understanding is always a partial understanding at best. This is especially true concerning the person of God. When God wishes to reveal himself to us, we are usually ill-equipped to receive the revelation. In order to begin a dialogue with human beings, God must be willing to begin with our misunderstanding of who we think he is.

Conclusion: God's Relationship With Human Beings

In beginning a dialogue with the ancient Hebrews, God met them in their understanding. Part of that understanding involved the idea of a scapegoat. That is, they needed some way to feel that they were worthy to come into the presence of a holy God. They imagined that the greatness of God precluded him from loving or even tolerating anything that was not perfect. Such a notion kept them at a distance from God. If they were to approach God, they would have to feel that they were somehow good in God's sight. Thus, a scapegoat, upon whom they could put all of their sin and guilt, was necessary in order for them to come into God's presence. Of course, God does not need a scapegoat to love us. Rather, we tend to use the scapegoat to approach God. In actuality, the scapegoat was not a necessity for God to approach us. For many of us,

Jesus is the scapegoat who allows us to approach a God who we think is otherwise unapproachable. Amazingly, Jesus is willing to be that scapegoat, particularly if that is what we need to come to God. The idea of the scapegoat, however, is not something God needs in order to come to us. Since God can maintain a relationship with human beings through pure forgiveness, Jesus may be our scapegoat, but he is not God's scapegoat. What separates us from God is not God's sense of justice but our sense of justice. Jesus is the scapegoat who bears our sin, not to appease God, but to appease our understanding so we may no longer fear God's presence.

No one comes to the Christian God except through the atoning work of Jesus, but if, because of our limited understanding, we need to believe that the atonement amounts to Jesus being our scapegoat in order for us to approach God, Scripture allows for such understanding. Equally, it allows us to see atonement as a matter of ransom or forgiveness, if that is what our understanding requires. God does not care much about the initial state of our understanding. Again, the full truth of what Jesus did on that cross goes far beyond our mind's ability to take in. Of course, some concepts of atonement may be more fruitful than others. Some concepts may enable us to come more fully into the Christian life than others, but, beyond that, God is not very interested in whether we have a correct understanding of atonement. God's desire is that we would have a concept of atonement that would allow us to enter a relationship with him so that, in time, he might reveal to us that he is more wonderful than we could think or imagine.

God's desire has always been that we would enter into relationship with him, but our human understanding of God has kept us from that relationship. We imagine that God is like us and can only love that which is beautiful and good, but God is not like us. He can love the unlovely. God even loves his enemies, and he tells us to do the same (see Matthew 5:44–45).

Unlike human beings who, for the most part, are incapable of forgiveness and demand payment from the guilty for their offense, God is capable of paying for the offense of the guilty through pure forgiveness. Since this is unfathomable to most of us, God allows us to conceive of Jesus on the cross as our scapegoat who allows us to approach an otherwise unapproachable God. God is more interested in our coming to him than our having a correct theological understanding. The postmodern critique tells us that an ultimate theological understanding is impossible since there is not an ultimate perspective open to human beings. This does not mean that our churches are devoid of meaning or that our theological tradition is false. Quite the contrary, we must realize that God meets us in many places, at many different points along our journey, and we must allow ourselves and others to be where we find ourselves in our relationship with God.

God is willing to work patiently within the limits of our understanding to accomplish his purposes. It makes little difference in our coming to God if we come by seeing Jesus' atonement as an act of pure forgiveness or the work of a scapegoat. What is important is that we see that it is because of what God has done and not because of what we have done.

Once we have entered into a relationship with God, however, our theological perspective does take on increased importance. Because God's purpose is not just that we come to him, but that we come to *know* him, and thereby be made like him, some theologies are more fruitful than others. The idea of a scapegoat may bring us to God, but it limits our understanding of God and ourselves.

It is easy to see how the idea of a scapegoat can give us a wrong picture of ourselves. When we commit some sin and put the blame on someone else, even for the sake of becoming lovable in God's sight, we deny a very important and real part of ourselves. More importantly, however, the idea of a scapegoat prevents us from getting a true picture of God. Instead, it gives us a picture of a god who is only able to love that which is lovely. We anthropomorphize God and imagine that his love is like our own.

By imagining that God is like ourselves, we certainly get a wrong picture of God and the nature of his love. Equally, such anthropomorphic notions of God also affect our idea of sin. Since we imagine that God's love is like our own, we imagine that sin is some kind of moral imperfection that God hates and, when present within us, is what causes God to separate himself from us. But God, unlike us, does not limit his affection to those who are good or beautiful. That may be the nature of human love, but Christ died for us while we were yet sinners (see Romans 5:8).

God's love sanctifies us and makes us beautiful but not as objects of love, as we commonly think. Rather, the perfection God desires for us is that we would experience his love in the midst of our sin and so become like him by loving those who do not seem lovable. Our sanctification occurs through our great transformation into agents of God's love.

It is only with such an understanding that we come to see our true selves and God. The only way we can understand the fullness of God's love and mercy is by understanding that our sin has not been put upon another but remains upon us, and yet it does not stop God from loving us or using us as his instruments to spread his love. It is only when we see ourselves as both saint and sinner, as ones who desire God's presence and yet constantly wander from it, that we truly realize who we are and the greatness of God's love for us.

> In my life I find that I am, in the classic phrase, *simul justus et peccator*, "both justified and a sinner." That is to say, I find that my life has been totally transformed by being one with Christ. And yet I still fall into the same old patterns of sin. This is not even a matter of percentages—for example, x-percent better, y-percent still sinful. Rather, I really am totally transformed, even on those days when I am just as much a sinner as if I were not redeemed at all. It is indeed puzzling how that should be possible, and yet I know it to be true.[10]

From the understanding of ourselves as both saint and sinner, and therefore forever in need of divine mercy and forgiveness, we are able to remain in a place of repentance from which to receive grace and the power to be transformed and made into God's likeness. The process of being made into God's likeness is also greatly aided by a better understanding of the divine nature, the focus of our next chapter.

Questions for Reflection

1. What is atonement? Compare and contrast ransom, satisfaction, and forgiveness theories of atonement.
2. Why did Jesus die on the cross?
3. What does Jesus' death teach us about God's love for us? What does it teach us about our love for one another?

8

Deep Concepts:
Substance, Relation,
and Identity

Our concept of God is no different from other concepts, at least insofar as it is shaped by a myriad of other concepts. Some of the important concepts that shape our idea of God, however, seem to be so basic to our understanding that we can easily come to believe that they must somehow be God-given. In actuality, however, even some of our most basic concepts are often the product of social conventions and human judgment drawn from our culture and language community. Such concepts may be the bedrock of our understanding, but our unreflective acceptance of them prevents the Spirit and the biblical text from having the power to renew our minds with more fruitful concepts. *Substance* is one such concept.

The origin of our idea of substance and the dominant place it holds in our thinking can be traced to Aristotle. Aristotle had claimed that to say that something is, or exists, has multiple meanings. Seven, blue, Paris, father, and tree, for example, may all be said to exist, but they exist in different ways. Seven exists as a quantity, while blue exists as a quality, Paris as a place, father as a relation, and tree as a substance, or thing in itself. The word *tree* is not a descriptor for anything other than tree; therefore, it is a primary substance. In the "Categories," Aristotle claimed that there are ultimately ten ways in which something can be said to exist. Of these ten categories, the most important to Aristotle was substance. His reasoning was that *substance* encompasses all of the other categories and their presuppositions.

> Everything except primary substances are either predicable of a primary substance or present in a primary substance.[1]

> There are several senses in which a thing is said to be first; yet substance is first in every sense—in definition, in order of knowledge, in time. For of the other categories, none can exist independently, but only substance.[2]

Anything other than substance is an *attribute*. For example, *the car* (substance) *is blue* (attribute). Or, *Robert* (substance) *is the father* (attribute) *of four children* (attributes of *father*, but substances in themselves). In scholastic thought, attributes were categorized as *genus, species, property, differentia*, and *accident*; in Aristotelian thought, they are *definition, genus, proprium*, and *accident* (see for example, Thomas Aquinas and Bonaventure of Bagnoregio [1221–1274]). Without delving into the details of attributes, it is safe to say that, for Aristotle, a primary substance is defined solely with respect to itself and not with respect to any other things. Only primary substance is independent of all else and, therefore, according to Aristotle, substance is most real. Substance has what Aristotle refers to as *whatness,* or an identity and definition (definiteness) that is lacking in other forms of existence that are not substance. Since other parts of speech (attributes) modify and describe, substance is most central to human language and understanding, and thus it must be what is ultimately real as well, or so Aristotle reasoned.

Most of us agree with Aristotle and view substance, or that which exists independent of all else, as that which is most real. This is especially true in regard to our individual identities. We seek to develop and maintain a substantial self—what we shall call *substantial identity*—whose identity and worth is independent of all else and therefore invulnerable to external circumstances or other people. Many people do not prefer to define themselves with respect to others—that is, they do not want to be attributes. By emphasizing their substantial identity, they create the illusion that independence will save them from whatever calamities might arise around them.

Conversely, many other people establish identities founded on relationships rather than private substance. In many African countries, for example, the people live according to a communalist axiom, whereby relationships with one another supersede individual identity. In opposition to Descartes' individualistic axiom (*Cogito ergo sum*, "I think therefore I am"), the African philosopher John S. Mbiti proclaimed, "I am because we are, and because we are, therefore I am."[3]

Many women also seem to gravitate toward relational rather than individualistic identities. There may be many factors that contribute to women's tendencies toward relational identities. There may be biological reasons, or her role as caregiver may also be a possible cause. The one common denominator, however, behind the tendency toward relational identities among women and certain other groups of people is a lack of access to the kind of wealth, power, and prestige needed to found a substantial identity. Without such access, the poor and disenfranchised (including many women) have no hope of establishing the illusion of a substantial identity and therefore find their identity in relationships. Such people have a very different perspective than those (usually rich males) who have a substantial identity.

One of the great insights of postmodern thought is that not only is our understanding perspectival, but we tend to privilege one element of certain binaries (two components of one thing) over others. For example, many privilege male perspectives over female, white people over people of color, and the rich over the poor. If that order were reversed and most people privileged the perspective of those who have been marginalized, our perception of our identity would be very different.

Traditional attempts to understand our own identity and the identity of God have been from an Aristotelian perspective, which privileges substance over relation. In simplistic terms, this perspective is male and rich rather than female and poor. If we were to consider identity from the marginalized perspective, which privileges relation over substance, we would see things very differently. Furthermore, such a marginalized perspective seems more compatible with the wisdom of contemporary social science and the teachings of Jesus.

Privileging Relationship Over Substance

Contemporary social science tells us that identity is always found in our relationship with others and not in ourselves. Our sense of self-worth and identity is mirrored through others. Other people reflect our identity back to us. We may wish or pretend to be independent of others with a self-made identity, insulated and invulnerable to forces outside ourselves, but according to contemporary research, such an identity is an illusion. Not surprisingly, Jesus seems to have been well aware of the relational nature of true identity.

Despite the fact that we generally perceive Jesus through the eyes of Western civilization, Jesus himself seems to consistently take the marginalized perspective. He was certainly out of sync with the dominant perspective of his day in that he consistently gave preference to women and he privileged the poor over the rich. The gospel accounts tell us that Jesus claimed to bring good news to the poor (see Luke 4:18), and that it was easier for a camel to go through the eye of a needle than for a rich man to enter the kingdom of heaven (see Matthew 19:24). Likewise, Jesus seems to privilege relation over substance in that he subordinates his own individual substance to his relation with the Father and the Spirit. His actions are not those of one who acts out of his own substance but out of relationship with the Father and the Spirit.

> "[T]he Son can do nothing on his own, but only what he sees the Father doing; for whatever the Father does, the Son does likewise" (John 5:19).

> "[I]f it is by the Spirit of God that I cast out demons, then the kingdom of God has come to you" (Matthew 12:28).

> "Those who speak on their own seek their own glory; but the one who seeks the glory of him who sent him is true, and there is nothing false in him" (John 7:18).

It seems strange that Jesus, who Christians profess to be God incarnate, claims to be powerless apart from a relationship with his Father. Perhaps this seems so strange to us because we imagine, like Aristotle, that the highest form of being, or what it means to be truly substantive, is to be independent of all else. Quite to the contrary, whatever claim Jesus makes to divinity seems based in relation rather than individual substance. Numerous passages of Scripture indicate his true source of identity.

> *"Do you not believe that I am in the Father and the Father is in me? The words that I say to you I do not speak on my own; but the Father who dwells in me does his works. Believe me that I am in the Father and the Father is in me; but if you do not, then believe me because of the works themselves"* (John 14:10–11).

> *"Yet even if I do judge, my judgment is valid; for it is not I alone who judge, but I and the Father who sent me"* (John 8:16).

> *"I can do nothing on my own. As I hear, I judge; and my judgment is just, because I seek to do not my own will but the will of him who sent me"* (John 5:30).

Jesus points to the fact that we are to be in a similar relationship with him, and therein find our ultimate identity and life.

> *"On that day you will know that I am in my Father, and you in me, and I in you"* (John 14:20).

What Jesus seems to stress, again and again, is that our true identity is in relation to God. Contrary to our Western attraction to independence or total autonomy, Jesus' way is often difficult to comprehend. Our perspective is generally that of Aristotle's, which privileges and sees as substantive that which is independent of all else. Jesus tells us that we will have life if we come to him (see John 5:40), but we find it difficult to heed such words because we think that we can find life in ourselves.

Of course, we can, with enough power and wealth, attempt to manipulate and control what others think about us and thus maintain the illusion of a substantial identity. Nevertheless, if we lose the power or wealth to support our illusion, our self-made identity quickly disintegrates. Even if we can maintain enough power and wealth to sustain the illusion for a lifetime, our mortality has a way of convincing us that our worth is not based on wealth, power, or prestige. On one's deathbed, no one ever regrets not having enough wealth or power to support the illusion of a substantial, independent identity. What we regret is not having spent more time with our spouses or children. What we regret is not having established better relationships. We regret the fact that our lives were more intent on developing the illusion of a substantial self than on developing relationships with those we loved.

Jesus understood that human identity was relational rather than substantive, and he tried to provide a model for such an identity. In the same way, however, because Jesus was both human and divine, he also provides us with a model for the divine identity as well. Like human identity, it too is an identity that privileges relation over substance.

The Identity of a Triune God

Many people today still look to medieval theology for an understanding of the Trinity. Many theologians—particularly from the era of high scholasticism (twelfth to fourteenth centuries)—used the Aristotelian distinction between substance and relation in their attempt to unravel the difficulties involved in understanding the identity of a triune God. The traditional formulas of the Christian doctrine of the Trinity presented a problem since it had always been maintained that each person of the Trinity (i.e., Father, Son, and Holy Spirit) was wholly God. Equally, those three persons were joined in the Godhead to create one God and not three. There would be no problem if each one of the three persons constituted a part of God, but Christian orthodoxy insisted that Jesus was wholly God and, equally, that the Father and the Holy Spirit were wholly God as well. As such, it seems that St. Patrick's analogy of the shamrock, with three leaves that constitute one shamrock, is not a proper analogy since it represents each person as a part of the whole rather than each being a whole in themselves.

One possible solution was to use the Aristotelian distinction between substance and relation. According to Aristotle, father and son are words that signify relations rather than substances. Father is a relation in that if one's children ceased to exist, one would no longer be a father, although there would be no change to them as a substance. Equally, once one's parents die, a person is no longer a daughter or son, although nothing has changed about their substance. If the persons of the Trinity were relations rather than substances, it would easily explain how three persons could come together to create a unitary God who was one substance but three relations. This was the solution offered by Boethius (480–524). Thomas Aquinas makes reference to Boethius in his own explanation of the Trinity but also notes Augustine, who held the contrary view that persons are substances. Aquinas quotes Augustine as saying,

> When we speak of the person of the Father, we mean nothing else but the substance of the Father, for person is said in regard to Himself, and not in regard to the Son.[4]

Aquinas' own position attempts to unite the positions of both Boethius and Augustine. He explains that the persons of the Godhead constitute a subsistent relation. He agrees with Boethius but points out that the relations that make up the Godhead are not like any other relations. All other relations are external to a substance and therefore accidental and not part of a thing's nature or essence. By contrast, the persons who make up the Godhead are relations that are essential and constitute the very nature of God and are therefore substantive as well.

There is another way to understand the triune God of Christianity, but it is one that most medieval theologians would have had trouble accepting because of their Aristotelian idea of substance as most real. The alternative explanation is that the persons of the Godhead are substances while the Godhead itself is a relation. That sounds like a heresy, since it would mean that the oneness of the Godhead was not a substance or that which was most real, but merely a relation. Of course, the reason it seems so heretical is that we have accepted the Aristotelian supposition that substance or "that which is independent of all else" is "most real." Aristotle had argued for that view, and the privileged (mostly male) founders of Western civilization advocated this dominant view.

Aristotle's arguments, however, are not as powerful as they once were. Today, we do not have the trust that the early and medieval Church had in language's ability to reflect objective reality. In our day, we find it difficult to see the kind of connection Aristotle imagined between language and reality, and we believe that language—and consequently our understanding, which is cast in language—is relative to culture and the judgments of human beings. So, the fact that our language privileges substance does not count for much. Today, more than ever before, we are in a position to question the privileged position that substance has enjoyed for so long. If we can consider theology from the feminist perspective and, with liberation theology—that is, the perspective of the poor—it seems natural that a relational rather than substantial theology is yet another perspective that might expand our understanding of God.

Fortunately, there is also a long theological tradition of the Trinity that is very similar to the way we are suggesting, although it has been somewhat marginalized for the past four hundred years. This perspective interpreted relation as more real than substance. It has its origins in Augustine (430), Pseudo-Dionysius (c. 500), Richard of St. Victor (1173), and Bonaventure (1274), and it is basically a theology of love.

This theology perceives God as a sort of divine lover, whereby the various elements of love are modeled within the Godhead itself. In order for God to be love, it is necessary for God to love his equal, for surely, as we learned above, love cannot be forced, coerced, or bought. Thus, if God is relational, another must have existed in God from the beginning of time. The incarnation of Jesus, then, represents the fulfillment of God's love for humanity (among many other things). But the relationship between the Father and Son is not enough. As Richard of St. Victor points out, love for another is incomplete unless it is directed outward. In other words, God cannot fully love the Son and vice versa without a sense of mission that is directed outward. Therefore, from the beginning of time, the Spirit existed in God as the outpouring of love between the Father and Son. In the end, God, as Father, Son, and Holy Spirit, models love for all creation. This relational triune God is perhaps best summed up in the concept, *perichoresis*. "*Perichoresis* means being-in-one-another."[5]

> *Perichoresis* expressed the idea that the three persons mutually inhere in one another, draw life from one another, "are" what they are by relation to one another.[6]

Such a concept provides a perspective from which we might get a much better insight into the nature of a God in whom individual substance is yielded to communion with the other persons of the Godhead. One of the most effective images used to communicate this idea of perichoresis is that of a divine dance. Catherine Mowry LaCugna (d. 1997) explains it beautifully.

There are neither leaders nor followers in the divine dance, only an eternal movement of reciprocal giving and receiving, giving again and receiving again. To shift metaphors for a moment, God is eternally begetting and being begotten, spirating and being spirated. The divine dance is fully personal and interpersonal, expressing the essence and unity of God. The image of the dance forbids us to think of God as solitary. The idea of trinitarian *perichoresis* provides a marvelous point of entry into contemplating what it means to say that God is alive from all eternity as love.[7]

This dance is what Jesus constantly demonstrates throughout the gospels. When he speaks of himself, it is always in relationship to the Father and the Spirit. Jesus reveals that relation is all important and most real. It is relation that is truly essential to the nature of God. As the theologian Leonardo Boff says, "Three Persons and a single communion and a single trinitarian community…is the best formula to represent the Christian God."[8]

By seeing the Godhead as a relational communion rather than a substance, we have a much better basis for understanding the mystery of the Trinity and a much better understanding of what it means to be made into God's likeness as human beings. By understanding the Godhead as a relational communion, the mystery of the Trinity is quite different from what we had imagined. It is still a mystery, but the mystery is not the result of contemplating something that defies the laws of thought. The fact that something defies logic is not the kind of mystery that fills us with awe and wonder. Logical mysteries simply stop us from thinking in that direction. The mystery of the Trinity is a different kind of mystery. It is a mystery that could capture our attention and fill us with wonder and awe forever. It is not an unknowable mystery but a mystery that is infinitely knowable.

The true mystery of the Trinity is this: how could three divine persons, with unlimited power and the capacity to be truly independent of all else, subordinate their own autonomous substance, in order to form the perfect relational union which is the Godhead? Within the triune God of Christianity there is the surrender of individual substance to a relationship with the other persons of the Godhead. This is a mystery to us because the subordination of substance to relation is so unlike anything human. Indeed, unlike human beings, the triune God of Christianity is able to value and maintain relation within the Godhead as supreme and above the substance of the individual persons of the Godhead. This is a mystery that fills us with awe and reveals to us just how very different the divine nature is from our own. As mysterious and unlike anything human as this is, however, God's desire is that we would become like him and surrender our own substance into the relationship that is God and his kingdom.

Of course, although this model for unity that the Godhead provides by privileging relation rather than substance has never been fully achieved (except in the life of Christ), that does not mean that it is an impossible model. It is like the star that we never reach but by which we set our course. Furthermore, by setting our course after such a model, the divine qualities open to us and begin to appear in our lives, albeit in limited fashion. Forgiveness, in particular, only becomes possible when we begin, in some minuscule way, to privilege relation over our own individual substance. Recall our earlier discussion of forgiveness and how rare it is among human beings. We see now that the reason for its rarity is that in order to forgive, one needs to be like God and privilege relation, and its preservation, over one's own individual substance. Few of us do that, and human existence, for the most part, is a substantial one. But it is this substantial existence that must come to an end so that we might come into the newness of life of which Jesus speaks.

A Twenty-First Century Perspective

Today we are in a better position to consider the possibility of relation, rather than substance, as being most real. Now that we know our ideas of substance and relation are culturally relative, and one has been marginalized while the other has become dominant because of human rather than divine decree, we are better able to change our perspective and see that relation rather than independence is most real. From such a perspective, the Godhead is most substantial, in the sense of being that which is most real, but not substantive in the sense of being independent of all else. Furthermore, the three independent persons who make up the Godhead are substances in the sense of being independent of all else. Thus, while the persons of the Trinity are substances and independent of all else, what is ultimately real is relation, and the Godhead is a relation rather than a substance.

There are some minor problems with this view that there are three separate persons in the form of independent substances that create *a* single relation, which is the Godhead. If three persons are in relation with one another, it would seem that they create three distinct relationships. That is, the relation of the Son to the Father (filiation), the Father to the Spirit (spiration), and the love between the Son and the Spirit. This may well be true, but the relation that comprises the Godhead is the inner unity that grounds the oneness of God. It is a meta-relation that unites all of the particular relational aspects into *one* love relationship and causes each person to submit his individual will to the oneness of the relation that exists between them. In fact, this might be what most typifies ideal love—the fact that a person's individual interest is subordinated, not to another person, but to a relationship with that person. In an ideal love, relationship and not the individual substance of lovers are most important and most real.

One of the things that separates Christian theology from all others is that it is neither purely monotheistic nor polytheistic. The Christian God is distinctly a relational God whose independent persons give us a picture of the ideal union that is to be found when one's own substance is subordinated to the greater reality of relation.

In the Sermon on the Mount and throughout the gospels, Jesus tells us that our real sin—what truly separates us from God—consists of all the things that fuel the false, substantial self. One of the central messages of the gospel is that if we would only turn from our lusts, anger, earthly treasure, worries, and judgments—things from which we try to draw identity and life—we would find that our true identity rests, not in increasing our substance with such things, but in our relationship to a God who loves us with a father's love. It is to this that we now turn and consider human nature and identity from the gospel perspective we have been developing throughout the preceding chapters.

Questions for Reflection

1. Describe the historical development of the concept of *substance*.
2. Compare and contrast *substance* and *relation*.
3. How does the Trinity redefine our understanding of God and one another?

9

Our Dual Nature:
Flesh and Spirit

At the beginning of the modern era, René Descartes claimed that human beings are composed of two substances: one body and the other, mind. Modernity inherited this Cartesian legacy, and the same dualism was applied to Scripture. Thus, for example, the Scriptural references to *flesh (sarx)* were often understood as merely "body," without reference to the nonphysical mind, spirit, or soul. In actuality, however, the term *flesh*, as it appears in the New Testament, is almost always metaphorical.

> *"[F]lesh and blood has not revealed this to you, but my Father in heaven"* (Matthew 16:17).

> *"For my flesh is true food and my blood is true drink"* (John 6:55).

Jesus is not referring to flesh in the literal sense. Paul's extensive use of the term is also metaphorical. Words that are used metaphorically can have multiple meanings. The word *cat*, for example, can have many meanings: "Raining cats and dogs," "cat burglar," or "cat-o'-nine-tails." The same is true with the word *flesh* in the New Testament. In the passage above from Matthew's Gospel the translators of the New International Version translate *"flesh and blood"* as "man." *For this was not revealed to you by man* (Matthew 16:17, NIV translation).

If *flesh and blood* means "man," what are we to make of John 6:55, where *flesh* and *blood* are "true food" and "drink"? It is very difficult to know the exact meaning of *flesh and blood* in this context, and people have been arguing over it for centuries. In any event, it appears evident that the term has different meanings. The difference is particularly evident when we compare Paul's use of *flesh* with his use of the term *spirit*.

As noted above, our modern legacy makes it easy for us to immediately disconnect body and soul. Thus, when *flesh* is found together with *spirit*, we perceive them as a metaphor for the material body in contrast to the immaterial soul or mind. It is easy to make such an assumption since our Western culture, even before Descartes and the modern period, had a long tradition of distinguishing mind from body. We find this in the Platonic tradition.

> Surely the soul can best reflect when it is free of all distractions such as hearing or sight or pain or pleasure of any kind….Then here too—in despising the body and avoiding it, and endeavoring to become independent—the philosopher's soul is ahead of all the rest.[1]

Such an elevation of mind above body was also at the base of Gnosticism (the assertion that a special knowledge, or *gnosis*, leads to salvation), but Paul does not seem to have been affected by either Platonic or Gnostic thinking. His concept of flesh seems very different from body, since the flesh (not the body) envies, hates, and practices sedition.

> *Now the works of the flesh are obvious: fornication, impurity, licentiousness, idolatry, sorcery, enmities, strife, jealousy, anger, quarrels, dissensions, factions, envy, drunkenness, carousing, and things like these* (Galatians 5:19–20).

Another possibility is to interpret *flesh* as it is contrasted with *spirit*, as "sinful nature" (see the NIV translation). This translation is as much a metaphor as the term *flesh*. It leaves us asking, what exactly is our sinful nature? Is it different or the same as the self? Does my sinful nature constitute the whole of my being or only a portion? If it is only a portion of my being, which portion?

In attempting to sort this out, we should recall that our sin, as we have said repeatedly, is not what causes God to separate himself from us, but rather what causes us to separate ourselves from God. We separate ourselves by identifying with the false sources of life and meaning of which Jesus warns us.

As noted above, our identity or notion of ourselves comes from what we identify with. If we identify with and try to find meaning and life in the things Jesus warns against, we will create a false, substantial self. I argue that this is the best way to understand the identity that Paul refers to as the *flesh*. By contrast, to live in the *spirit* is to live at the core of our being. It is to live out of our real self, to be who we are *in relationship to* God. It is to live as if we are loved by God because we are his beloved daughters and sons. Before we did anything right or wrong, we were his creation, and he loved us because we were his. Our true self is rooted in God's love, not because of the greatness of our prayers or almsgiving, nor our ability to keep our oaths or make good judgments, but simply because of God's loving nature. Our actions may be the things that cause other people to love us, but God's love is not like human love, as we have previously seen. As a matter of fact, the good things we do (prayers, oaths, and so forth) can be the very things that can keep us from God, since we can easily come to identify with them rather than the fact that we are God's beloved daughters and sons. That is, we can live in the flesh rather than the spirit.

Jesus teaches us to live as he lived. He lived with God in all of his thoughts. He did not identify with, nor allow himself to be occupied by, those things that he warns us of in the Sermon on the Mount. Instead he lived his life in a constant awareness that he was the beloved son of God. He tells us to follow him by assuming the same filial relationship with God. We, however, do not live as sons and daughters of God because we choose to live in the flesh and attempt to establish a substantial identity by finding life and meaning in things that satisfy our earthly desires. Remember, one of the essential characteristics of love is attention, and we all too easily fix our attention on worry, lust, anger, or good reputation. As we love such things and give our attention to them, we no longer live in the spirit but in the flesh. Once again, we can say with conviction that what separates most people from God (that is, their sin) is that they spend a trivial existence identifying with and attempting to find life and meaning in something other than God.

Sin and righteousness are essentially a matter of belonging. God desires that we all come to righteousness and that we understand that we belong to him and not the world and its gods. In order to find righteousness, and thus live in the spirit rather than the flesh, two things are essential. One is a willingness to live in an almost constant state of repentance or turning away from the false gods that so easily and quickly turn our attention away from God. The second essential is a desire and ability to live in a state of poverty.

Poverty as Key to Living in the Spirit

Throughout the gospel, there is a definite preference for the poor. The gospel is *good news* to the poor (see Luke 4:18), and the poor are the *blessed* (see Matthew 5:3). By contrast, the rich seem cursed, and we are told that it was easier for a camel to go through the eye of a needle than for a rich man to enter the kingdom of heaven (see Matthew 19:24). In the parable of the prodigal son, poverty is the great blessing that forces the son back to his father's arms. Imagine his state if he had never fallen into poverty. The son may have remained separated from his father forever.

This poverty, which is so essential to the Christian life, is not simply a poverty of wealth and possessions, but a poverty of power and prestige as well. It is quite literally the poverty of the lower class. Francis of Assisi (1811–1226) understood that one of the keys to living the Christian life was to offer your entire life to God, including your possessions. Francis interpreted this call to mean that he should own nothing, including clothes and a place to rest his head. Franciscans are thus known as the *Order of Friars Minor* (that is, the "Order of Lesser Brothers"). Not surprisingly, humility and poverty became the hallmarks of Franciscan life. We learn from them—and from the gospels—that it is so dangerous to possess wealth because it entails many things that allow for the creation of the false self.

According to Max Weber (1864–1920), a person's social class is established by some combination of wealth, power, or prestige. The upper class is constituted of people who have enormous wealth, power, and prestige; the middle class is composed of people with moderate amounts of wealth, power, and prestige; and the lower class is made up of people who have little or no wealth, power, or prestige. We live in a culture driven by success and the quest for more material gain. The journey up the ladder of success, however, is the very thing that leads us away from a life in the spirit and simply adds to the illusions of the flesh. Our identity becomes less focused on God as we gain more wealth, power, and prestige. Of course, the poor, who have little or no wealth, power, or prestige, could lust after such things and identify with them even in their absence. Equally, it is possible for someone with considerable means to be "poor in spirit," and identify with nothing but that fact that they are God's beloved. Jesus is our model of poverty.

Christians believe that Jesus is God incarnate. Everything was ultimately his, yet he chose to possess nothing. At any moment, he could have called upon legions of angels to change the circumstances of his life to whatever he wished, and yet he chose to live out of powerlessness. If he displayed his power and demonstrated his ability to use force in order to make others do what he wanted, his fame would have surpassed any emperor or modern-day rock star. He chose instead a poverty of wealth, power, and prestige so that, in the absence of such things, his identity would be totally in God. That is, his identity was (and is) based exclusively on his relationship with his heavenly Father. He resisted the fleshly identity that comes from idolatry and lived instead in the Spirit or at the core of his being as God's beloved son. He challenges us to follow him and live in that same Spirit.

As fallen humans, we are constantly tempted to sin, to look away from God. When Satan tempted Jesus, he was asking him to look away from his source of identity, luring him into the wealth, power, and prestige of the world. Jesus was tempted to turn stones into bread (see Matthew 4:3) and to throw himself down from the pinnacle of the temple to demonstrate his power as the son of God (see Matthew 4:5–6). He was told that he could have *all the kingdoms of the world and their splendor* (Matthew 4:8) if he would just turn from his Father and worship the prince of this world. All the wealth and prestige imaginable could have been his, but Jesus knew that such wealth, power, and prestige would distract him from his focus on our Father.

Many of us have the illusion that by satisfying all of our human lusts, acquiring all the earthly treasure we desire, crushing all of our enemies, and having everyone respect our good deeds and judgments, we can create for ourselves an ideal identity and thus acquire ultimate happiness. The truth, however, is that creating such an identity is to live in the flesh rather than the Spirit. It amounts to living on the surface of our being where every vicissitude determines, from moment to moment, who we are and who we think we should become. We need to live at a deeper level, where our identity and character are immune to the circumstances that so enormously affect the flesh. Once again, we must learn that we are God's beloved daughters and sons, and that God is *our Father* from whose love nothing can separate us. When our identity is founded on this core, and we live at this level, we are invulnerable to the "slings and arrows of outrageous fortune."[2]

Jesus was the only person who ever truly realized an identity that was founded purely with respect to his relationship with God. He alone completely rejected an earthly, fleshly identity in favor of a heavenly one. Unlike us, Jesus never sinned. He may have been tempted with an earthly identity, but he never succumbed. Even when he felt that God had abandoned him (see Matthew 27:46 and Mark 15:34), it was still to God that he committed his spirit (see Luke 23:46).

We are called to follow him and walk the path that Jesus has prepared for us. The ideal of the Christian life is to set our gaze continually upon God, just like Jesus. Of course, that is impossible, and we all fail to live exactly like Jesus. The good news, however, is that we simply need to repent and return to God's presence every time we find ourselves attempting to draw life and meaning from things apart from God. Since we so easily wander from God's presence and are in almost constant need of repentance, we will eventually realize that God's abiding presence in our lives is the result of his forgiveness and grace, and not our own ability to make ourselves like Jesus.

It is very easy to be kept from the knowledge of God and the fullness of life he has for us. One very common way is to think that other things are more essential than following Jesus and living in continual awareness of God's presence through repentance and forgiveness. A recent bestseller claims that our central purpose in life is to worship God. Worship is certainly essential to the Christian life. Indeed, without worship of God, we very quickly come to worship ourselves. But the belief that worship is the paramount purpose of the Christian life can deceive us into believing that by worshiping God, we have done what is most important. If we see worship as our main purpose, we will be tempted to think that by worshiping Jesus we can have the fullness of life he promises without following him. Furthermore, the more we worship Jesus as God, the less we can expect ourselves to follow him as the model for what it means to be human. Jesus is worthy of worship, but when we make our worship of him the center of our faith, it can be a very clever way to avoid following him. Surely, worship is more appealing than following. Worship demands little in the way of surrender; following him demands that we surrender everything. Jesus leads us into poverty, where God alone is our treasure, where God alone is present.

Jesus offers us true salvation through God alone. In the end, salvation is not a matter of being saved from hell or an eternal torturer, but a matter of being saved from all of the false gods of this world that deceive us into directing our hope away from God.

Questions for Reflection

1. What does it means to *live in the flesh?*
2. Compare and contrast "living in the flesh" and "living in the spirit."
3. What role should worship play in our faith?
4. What does it mean to surrender everything to God?

10

Saved From What?

Jesus often refers to being "saved." In Luke 18:42 he says, "*your faith has saved you.*" In this case, the man has been given his sight, and it is easy to interpret being *saved* as simply being rescued from blindness (see Luke 18:35–42). In other places, however, it is more difficult to recognize what Jesus is saving us from. In Luke 8:5–12, for example, Jesus tells a parable about seed being scattered on different soil. Here, the seed is the Word of God, says Jesus. When the seed (the Word) falls upon the soil (humanity), the devil "*takes away the word from their hearts, so that they may not believe and be saved.*" In Mark's Gospel, we are told that "*the one who believes and is baptized will be saved*" (16:16). And John's Gospel tells us that "*God did not send the Son into the world to condemn the world, but in order that the world might be saved through him*" (3:17). Later in the Gospel of John, Jesus says, "*I say these things that you may be saved*" (5:34) and "*I am the gate. Whoever enters by me will be saved, and will come in and go out and find pasture*" (10:9). Jesus' most frequent statement concerning being saved is "*the one who endures to the end will be saved*" (Matthew 10:22 and 24:13; and Mark 13:13). It is difficult to discern from these passages exactly what we are being saved from.

Many believe that being saved means going to heaven and being saved from hell, but Jesus never says that. It is quite natural, however, that our initial concept of being saved involves escaping punishment.

When we first become aware of God's presence in our lives, we know very little. As explored previously, our first notion of God resembles our parents more than anything else. If we are older when we first become seriously aware of God, our initial idea may be a composite of several human authorities. From such experiences it is easy for us to believe that being saved amounts to avoidance of punishment brought on by our disobedience. Punishment often follows from disobedience to human authority, so it is quite natural to expect the same from God. With this expectation, we seek some way to be saved from this punishment.

There is nothing wrong with this rationale since our initial understanding of God, or any other person for that matter, is always a wrong understanding, or at least a very limited understanding. Such a wrong or limited understanding is the initial basis for any relationship. In order for our relationship with God to become a loving one, we must move beyond our preconceived interpretation of authority. Some never do.

Some people maintain that salvation is a matter of being one of the elect who are spared from punishment by professing a correct theological doctrine or maintaining a certain religious practice. For many, salvation is a matter of simply professing the word, *Jesus*.

> *"Everyone who calls on the name of the Lord shall be saved"* (Acts 2:21).

> *[I]f you confess with your lips that Jesus is Lord and believe in your heart that God raised him from the dead, you will be saved* (Romans 10:9).

Jesus himself, however, does not seem to put much stock in the mere use of his name.

> *"On that day many will say to me, 'Lord, Lord, did we not prophesy in your name, and cast out demons in your name, and do many deeds of power of your name?' Then I will declare to them, 'I never knew you; go away from me, you evildoers'"* (Matthew 7:22–23).

Although Jesus does not seem to put much stock in the use of his name, he does indicate the importance of being known by him. His knowing us seems to be the key issue. In order to be known by him, we must become his followers—his disciples—who are intimately known by him and thus eventually become like him.

Theological insight does not necessarily mean that we are known by Jesus. Some may believe that a correct theological understanding of God causes us to find favor with him, and, as a consequence, he therefore decides not to punish us. It is not, however, that we find favor with God by believing the right things, but rather that by following Jesus, and becoming his disciples he imparts to us a right understanding of God. We are saved from a wrong understanding of who God is, and therein we find the fullness of life God has for us.

Thus, salvation is something that happens in us and not in God. We are the ones who need to be saved from our wrong concept of God. God has always known that we are his beloved daughters and sons; we are the ones who need this revelation. So salvation represents a change in our phenomenal reality or reality as we understand it. By being converted and saved from a wrong concept of God, we encounter a new reality. With our conversion we come to understand that God is behind our experience and that he loves us with the love of a perfectly benevolent and wise parent who wishes to lead his children into the fullness of life.

Of course, we do not step into this reality in a magical moment of conversion. The salvation that Jesus offers is a transformative process. It may feel magical at first, but true conversion requires time. The transformation between human-centered reality and God-centered reality can be compared to the change in direction of a long locomotive: at first it whines and hisses, screeching to a slow, laborious halt. Then, slowly, its gears are redirected and it moves in the opposite direction. Similarly, it takes time to recognize and turn away from sin. It takes a considerable journey to strip the linguistic, cultural, and philosophical influences that have shaped us. In short, knowing God requires effort, time, patience, and God's grace. We can accept revelation in an instant; living it takes a lifetime.

As explored above, the process of conversion may begin with a belief that we are being saved from punishment, but after we have walked a distance with God, it becomes evermore difficult to maintain that belief. Our understanding changes over time, or at least it should change, as our experience informs and corrects our understanding. This should especially be the case with our understanding of salvation and our idea of what it is from which we are being saved. As we continually experience God's mercy and grace, the idea of God as the great punisher of disobedience from whom we must be saved begins to fade. The idea of God as an eternal torturer is undermined by years of experiencing God's presence in our lives, despite our all-too-frequent rejection of him. As we reverse our engines, we begin to see that Jesus' mention of being saved is ultimately a matter of being saved from our own blindness concerning the greatness of God's love and mercy. As Bonaventure says, life is a process of emanation and return—we are created by God (we emanate from the Father) and thus with God's grace and forgiveness continually return to God.

The revelation brought by Jesus also saves us from much of the sin that consumes the lives of so many. Indeed, as we come to understand the God of the universe as our own Father, worry no longer occupies us. Equally, earthly treasure and worldly lusts grow dim in the light of knowing that we are God's beloved.

As we come to better know God, our understanding or prejudice concerning hell also changes. We realize that hell, or our separation from God, results from our refusal to turn from our identification with the things of this world. Note that hell should *not* be equated with the things of this world, but rather, our *identification* with the things of this world, and our refusal to relinquish that identity in order that our flesh might die and we might come to live in the spirit.

The solution or salvation that Jesus offers to avoid such a hell is simply to repent, or turn away from the idols of this world, and accept God's forgiveness and restoration. In order to receive salvation, we must believe the revelation that Jesus brings. To receive salvation, we must come to realize that (1) we have separated ourselves from God in order to pursue other gods, and (2) God is willing to suffer for our offense—and all the evil or destruction that our separation from him entails—to restore us as his beloved. In short, we must come to believe that God's love is greater than our sin.

For salvation, we must do as Jesus says and endure to the end (see Matthew 10:22 and 24:13; and Mark 13:13). As we saw, this is Jesus' most frequent reference to being saved. The process by which we "endure to the end" is one of almost constant repentance. To remain in God's presence, or rather to remain *aware of* God's presence, we need to constantly turn from the gods of this world that so easily capture our attention and keep us from an awareness of his presence. It is our awareness of his presence that transforms us into his likeness, and an awareness of his presence is always entered into through repentance for not having stayed in his presence.

This does not mean that we initiate a forgiving response from God with our repentance. God's forgiveness is not in response to our repentance, but precedes our repentance, just as the forgiveness of the prodigal's son's father precedes his son's repentance: *While he was still far off, his father saw him and was filled with compassion* (Luke 15:20–21).

Just as the father in the parable has compassion and his forgiveness precedes his son's repentance and request for forgiveness, so it is with God and our approach for forgiveness. Despite the fact that God's forgiveness precedes our repentance, repentance is still necessary. Our human reality is, for the most part, perceptual, and if we do not perceive God's forgiveness, it does not become a part of our reality. In other words, it is not so much a matter of whether or not God forgives us, but whether we are aware of that forgiveness. Without repentance by which we turn from our false gods, God's forgiveness goes unnoticed, and we remain in our hellish existence serving gods who consume us.

Repentance must be constant and ongoing; it is the very thing that bring us into an awareness of God's presence and ultimately transforms us into his likeness. We must live in a constant state of repentance due to the sinister nature of sin and the fact that we so easily fall under its sway. Sin—our identification with anything other than God—can slip into our lives unnoticed. Even when it is noticeable, it can appear innocuous. Sin can take such possession of our awareness that it commands our focus—redirects our attention away from God—and we can see nothing else. This is why it is so important to repent and turn from these idols before they take such total possession of us that we no longer have any desire or inclination to turn from them.

Salvation, then, from our limited perspective, seems to be a process that begins with the belief that God is our loving Father and we are his beloved daughters and sons. As we continue to keep this belief at the center of our lives, as Jesus had, and repent and turn whenever we find something else becoming our source of life and identity, we find ourselves being made evermore into the likeness of God's son. Salvation is a matter of being saved from all the lesser existences or hells that result from failing to achieve a deeper understanding of our ultimate union with God. Thus, we are saved from our illusions of reality, and salvation leads us to an

> ...[a]uthentic human existence as it is determined in Jesus Christ....

> ...[A]uthentic human existence is that form of existence which echoes the Yes uttered by the Son to the Father from all eternity, and which echoes the pattern of humanity-for-others exhibited in his incarnate existence. It is this form of existence, this life-content which is the *telos* of election.[1]

Jesus' "Yes" is the truth of the gospel! More importantly, however, his "Yes" is the beauty of the gospel as well. One of the great sins of modernity was to convince us that truth was all important and beauty was something that could seduce us and lead us away from objective truth. But contrary to what modernity led us to believe, it is the beauty of the gospel that is first and foremost, and it is the beauty of the gospel that leads us into a love relationship with God. The next chapter considers the beauty of the gospel and its transformative power.

Questions for Reflection

1. What does it mean to be saved?
2. What hinders or helps our journey toward God?
3. What role does repentance play in salvation?

11

Beauty and Truth

As previously explored, part of the legacy inherited from modernity has been the idea that we are only to believe that which is true. For many modernists, this is an ultimate moral obligation. The consequence of this theory is that in order to believe in God we must first have evidence for the truth of God's existence.

Early in the last century, William James (1842–1910) contradicted his modernist peers by claiming that the acquisition of substantial evidence for belief begins through belief itself, with very little or no evidence. Very often, says James, only faith in a particular belief can open the possibility for evidence.

> There are, then, cases where a fact cannot come at all unless a preliminary faith exists in its coming. *And where faith in a fact can help create the fact*, that would be an insane logic which should say that faith running ahead of scientific evidence is the "lowest kind of immorality" into which a thinking being can fall. Yet such is the logic by which our scientific absolutists pretend to regulate our lives![1]

Like a postmodern thinker, William James seems correct in his criticism of the scientific mentality that demands evidence prior to belief. Indeed, the very nature of a scientific hypothesis requires us to accept a belief prior to evidence. Of course, the defenders of the modern, scientific mentality would argue that a scientific hypothesis is only loosely held and will be abandoned if evidence to support the belief does not immediately follow. But the history of science includes numerous examples of adherence to scientific hypotheses long past the point of being reasonable, and many of these "irrational" hypotheses did eventually find the evidence they sought.

Although we often romanticize such tenacity and view it as courageous, in actuality such persistence is often inspired more by ego or an inability to admit error. For many people, religious beliefs may also be grounded in the ego or narrow-mindedness, but there is another possible ground for religious beliefs. Indeed, it is possible to hold a religious belief because of the beauty we find in the object of our faith. Often the object of one's faith creates a sense of the sublime, which is capable of lending support to the belief. There is usually no internal bell that rings to tell us that something is true, but there is such a bell when we recognize something as divinely beautiful. This sense of divine beauty is what lies at the base of the Christian faith. It is not founded upon the truth of the existence of some creator and ruler of the universe; rather, it is founded upon the beauty we find in the God that Jesus reveals. The beauty of the gospel is primary, not only in the sense that it is often what first draws us to God, but also in the sense that it overwhelms us, enchants us, fascinates us, and calls us in ways that the truth never can.[2]

I know a man who, as a nominal Jew, had no interest in the gospel. One day in a taxi cab ride to the airport, the cab driver asked if he had ever read the New Testament. My friend said no but accepted a pocket edition of the New Testament when the cab driver offered it. He eventually read it out of curiosity. Afterward he thought to himself, "I don't believe a word of this, but it is exactly who I would want God to be." He began to weep uncontrollably. It was not the truth of the gospel that began his faith journey but the beauty of the gospel.

Beauty as the Cornerstone of Faith

Some of us begin our journey of faith by believing in the truth of the gospel, but even then, it is the beauty of the gospel that ultimately becomes the cornerstone of our faith. Since the Christian faith is, at its base, a love relationship with God, we must first see (or feel, touch, or hear) the lovability of God. Access to God's love is not found in the truth of his existence, but the beauty of his existence. To merely accept the truth of God's sovereignty over the universe, without any real love for him and the way he does things, is to respond to God like a demon. The demons that Jesus encounters in the gospels seem to know the truth of who Jesus is—they even obey his commands. Their rebellion against God is not rooted in their not knowing the truth, but their lack of seeing the beauty in the way God does things. A demon knows the truth of God's existence, but does not see the beauty of God's love and forgiveness. Nor does a demon see the beauty of God's meekness and God's willingness to pay for the sins of those who appear to be so undeserving. The demons' failure to see the beauty of the gospel—that is, to really know God—is the basis of their rebellion.

Many human beings are in a demonic state. They accept the fact of God's existence and sovereignty, but they do not like the way he does things. Therefore they separate themselves from God's kingdom, and thus God's love. God is looking for people who are the polar opposite of demonic creatures: people who may have very little evidence to support the fact that the God that Jesus reveals rules the universe, but their hope is that he does because of the great beauty they see in that revelation. God sent his son to reveal to us the beauty of his existence so that whoever had eyes to see might fall in love with the God that Jesus reveals.

God does not desire that we merely believe in his existence and blindly obey his commands. If God expected a robotic response to his love for us, he would have made his existence and power much more evident, and he would have limited our options for sin. God desires people who fall in love with him because of the great beauty they find in what Jesus reveals about God's nature. For example, God is like the father of the prodigal son (see Luke 15:11–32); God has prepared a banquet for all who have no better place to be (see Luke 14:16–24); God assures us that the one who comes to him in the last hour gets the same reward as the one who has labored all day (see Matthew 20:1–16); and God's kingdom is a precious pearl, in the light of which everything else is worthless (see Matthew 13:45–46).

Of course, without being fully converted, we do not see the God that Jesus reveals as beautiful. We may get some initial glimpses of God's beauty, but without being fully converted, we continue to think that the laborer who comes in the last hour should not receive the same payment as those who have labored all day (see Matthew 20:1–16). We believe that the older brother of the prodigal son is right to resent his brother and to resent his father's refusal to punish him (see Luke 15:11–32). And we certainly do not believe that Jesus really meant that we are to love our enemies (see Matthew 5:44; Luke 6:27). Without a deep conversion, we simply fail to see the beauty in the God that the gospel reveals. Sadly, we think it will be enough if we acknowledge God's existence and obey his commandments, and thus we fall short of the conversion God has prepared for us. If we fail to recognize the beauty of these divine images and believe that it is enough to acknowledge a creator and ruler of the universe to whom we are obedient, we will not be ready for his kingdom.

I once asked someone who considered himself a very faithful Christian what he would do if he found that Satan rather than God was the true sovereign of the universe. His reply was that he would serve whoever was the true sovereign of the universe. For him, beauty and goodness were not part of the equation. It was merely a matter of serving whoever was the true ruler of the universe, rather than a love relationship based on the beauty of a divine lover.

It is not surprising that people feel this way since our modern mind has privileged truth above beauty and goodness. In the ancient world, the beautiful and the true were inseparably connected. For Plato, the ideal form of a thing possessed the highest level of truth and thus it was also the most beautiful. And for Aristotle the beautiful, the good, and the true were intrinsically intertwined within the human condition. With the Modern period, however, these three elements, so essential to the human condition, were separated and truth was privileged above the other two.

Modern Thought and the Privileging of Truth

There is no single historical reason for the separation and subsequent privileging of truth over beauty and goodness. The process was slow and gradual with many contributing factors. The increasing institutionalization of medieval Christianity did much to start the process. As Christianity struggled to interpret God's method of speaking through Scripture and tradition, ritual practice and trust in God was increasingly transformed into a set of orthodox beliefs and rubrics. With the Reformation, and the idea of *sola Scriptura* (Scripture alone), the Word was interpreted as the only important truth, and as a consequence the Reformationists set out to destroy artistic images and rituals that were originally intended to portray the beauty of the faith and Scripture. The words of many Reformation thinkers were not poetic words intended to evoke in us a sense of beauty, but they were produced to provide a comprehensive and exact doctrinal understanding. In the Modern period, this movement toward a more narrow and precise theological interpretation, devoid of feeling, became the norm for the new science. With Descartes and Newton, mathematics became the paradigm for understanding the world. Beauty was relegated to the realm of the imagination, very much removed from truth. The truth was no longer beautiful but a matter of brute facticity.

The science of modernity taught us to believe that no matter how beautiful something is, if it is not true, we should not believe it; and if it is true, its beauty is of no consequence. Beauty came to be seen not as something inseparably tied to truth, but as something that could seduce us and lead us away from the truth. Thus, in our understanding of the biblical revelation, many Christians sought only the truth of the revelation and paid no mind to its beauty.

> What has happened to us, as human beings first of all, and then as Christians, that we do not see it as something sublimely obvious that the biblical revelation…is somehow related to *beauty*.[3]

We have been seduced, not by superstition, as was the fear of modernity, but by a scientific mentality that claimed to protect us from error. The science of modernity insisted that the naked truth of objective facts is what we should be seeking. We now know that bare facts are an illusion, and that a narrow and precise mathematical understanding does not always facilitate our understanding of the reality of the human condition.

Similarly, the Reformation idea of *sola Scriptura,* which supposed that we had the ability to correctly interpret the words of Scripture, has become increasingly difficult to defend. In light of the past two centuries and our increased understanding of the nature of language, history, and culture, we now know that words and facts need to be interpreted, and we can never be sure if our interpretation is what God intends. Fortunately, however, we are not abandoned and left with only our own interpretation of truth.

The Beauty of the Gospel

Thankfully, our access to the gospel is not totally dependent on our ability to know narrow or precise truths. There is also an aesthetic path that requires little in the way of interpretation. Often the beautiful images of the gospel simply strike us with an emotive, noncognitive sense of awe. These images need not be interpreted solely through doctrines and theology. Rather, we can simply let them produce a sense of the divine deep within us.

One image that particularly strikes me with such a sense of divine beauty is that of Jesus washing the feet of his disciples, the last thing he does before his death and resurrection. It was a Jewish custom to welcome people into one's home by having their feet washed. A typical task for gentile servants (and certainly not the master of the house), washing feet was considered too unclean and humiliating for Jews, even for Jewish servants. But the last act of Jesus with his followers is to wash their feet—even the feet of Judas! Love your enemies! What a beautiful image of the love of God. What a beautiful image of who God is calling us to be as his followers.

Similarly, the image of Jesus on the cross, and his response to torture by praying for forgiveness for those who were torturing him, gives us a powerful image of divine beauty. Many of the parables also present us with such images. The story of the prodigal son, like so many other parables, does not provide us with a basis for resolving theological problems or paradoxes, but it does teach us about our relationship with God. What is most essential to the Christian life is that we fall in love because we recognize something divinely beautiful about the God that the gospels reveal. The things that Jesus did and the parables of which he spoke are well suited to that purpose.

A Place for Truth

Although beauty plays a primary role in the transmission and reception of faith, truth also has a place in our spiritual journey. Truth is critical, but it follows beauty, not only in the sense that the beauty of the gospel is what often first attracts us to the Christian life, but also because the only real evidence for the truth of the gospel comes after we have dared to follow Jesus and have experienced the same faithful, heavenly Father that he experienced. Truth, then, is important, but it follows from our love for what we see as beautiful within God through Jesus. Thus objective truth is *not* the ultimate basis for belief.

William James once claimed that there are two great philosophical imperatives: "We must know the truth; and we must avoid error."[4] Of these two principles, the scientific community under modernity established the avoidance of error as a great maxim for life. That is, above all else, say the modernists, we are to avoid error. Accordingly, we are expected to accept nothing without evidence or sufficient warrant. James, on the other hand, privileged the pursuit of truth, claiming that our fear of error could actually keep us from the truth. This is certainly the case in regard to Christianity.

> When I look at the religious question as it really puts itself to concrete men, and when I think of all the possibilities which both practically and theoretically it involves, then this command that we shall put a stopper on our heart, instincts, and courage, and *wait*—acting of course meanwhile more or less as if religion were not true—til doomsday, or till such time as our intellect and senses working together may have raked in evidence enough—this command, I say seems to me the queerest idol ever manufactured in the philosophic cave....But if we are empiricists, if we believe that no bell in us tolls to let us know for certain when truth is in our grasp, then it seems a piece of idle fantasticality to preach so solemnly our duty of waiting for the bell. Indeed, we *may* wait if we will,...but if we do so, we do so at our peril....[5]

Indeed, in many areas of life, if we choose not to believe until we have sufficient evidence, the evidence will never come. This is certainly the case with the Christian life. The truth of the gospel is only revealed as we trust that God will do for us what he did for Jesus. The evidence for such a belief can only follow—and never precede—belief. Evidence spawns from our captivation with the beauty of the gospel that inspires us to follow Jesus. We become aware of a presence that is not our own. We become more sensitive and aware of divine purposes, and we begin to recognize an order to our lives that we did not create. When we fall in love with Jesus and begin to follow him, we come into the fullness of the life that he promises, we come into Christian faith. There is no need for further evidence. Christian faith is not supported by some objective, measurable truth; rather, faith is subjective, creating peace and joy that fills our soul because of our ever-greater experience of the beauty of the gospel.

There is, however, more to the Christian life than the peace and joy that comes from our increasing awareness of the beauty of the gospel. There is also happiness. But happiness, like so many of our other concepts, is in serious need of being reconsidered from a gospel perspective rather than the perspective of our culture.

Questions for Reflection

1. What is beauty? What is truth?
2. How can beauty lead to truth?
3. Can we identify that which is most beautiful? Explain.

12

Happiness:
A Postmodern End

Despite the fact that we all claim to desire happiness, most of us have hardly any notion of its meaning. Generally, our concept of happiness tends to be little more than some vague notion of momentary pleasure or contentment. Such vague interpretations of happiness are not compatible with the gospel life. Fortunately, in addition to our present vague notions of happiness, Aristotle offers a much richer notion of happiness and one which I think is more compatible with the gospel.

For Aristotle, happiness was tied to the idea of change. Whenever anything changes, we can speak of four possible causes for the change: material, formal, efficient, and final. For example, imagine the construction of a home. If we were inquiring about the material cause, we would cite the bricks, cement, and wood. Such material was certainly the *cause* of the house coming into existence. But we could also ask what caused the house to take its specific shape. To answer that question we would have to cite the *formal* cause or the blueprints. In order to discover how the formal cause became a reality, we would turn to the masons and carpenters as the *efficient* cause. Lastly, Aristotle identified the *final* or *teleological* cause: For what purpose was the house built? In the case of a home, the final cause would be that someone needed a place to live.

In his understanding of the natural world, Aristotle believed that the final cause was the most important of the causes. According to Aristotle, every living thing had a purpose. Things moved toward their *telos* (that is, the purpose or end that nature had preordained for them). If such ends did not exist, for example, then some acorns might become oaks, and others might become pine trees or things other than trees entirely. The reason acorns always move toward becoming oak trees is because they possess an end that prevents them from becoming anything else. In Aristotle's thinking, a chicken comes from the egg of a hen because its purpose is established before conception. Otherwise, eggs would be free to develop in any way. The fact that all eggs (or at least all chicken eggs) move toward becoming chickens speaks of a specific end that has been established for the egg. So, although this world is in a constant state of flux, there is an intelligible order to the changes we observe in nature.

The idea of final cause runs throughout all of Aristotle's thinking, but it is perhaps most interesting in regard to his interpretation of human action. According to Aristotle, the final cause of all human action—that is, the end toward which we all move—is happiness. Human beings always act for a purpose, and although they all act differently, the ultimate purpose or end of all human action is happiness. We may do certain things for the sake of health or wealth, honor or pleasure, but in so doing, we ultimately strive toward happiness. Happiness is always an end, and never a means. In other words, we do not seek to be happy to gain wealth or honor. Happiness may be the fruit of wealth or honor, but wealth and honor are not the fruit of happiness. Happiness is the ultimate end.

Aristotle demonstrates his theory with the example of bridle making, which is not done for its own sake, but for the sake of horsemanship, which in turn is not done for its own sake, but for the sake of being good at war. Even being good at war, however, is not done for its own sake but in order to live at peace. Of course, the desire to live at peace is for the purpose of being happy, but being happy has no higher good. It is the *summa bonum* or "highest good." "Happiness, then, is something final and self-sufficient, and is the end of action."[1]

Happiness, says Aristotle, is not something that can be realized in some moment of bliss but is the end of a process, much like the way an oak generates over time from an acorn. For Aristotle, human happiness is achieved over a lifetime. "One swallow does not make a summer, nor does one day; and so too one day, or a short time, does not make a man blessed and happy."[2]

For this reason, Aristotle says that a young man cannot be truly happy at a young age: "...boys who are called happy are being congratulated by reason of the hopes we have for them."[3] Thus, it may be said that they are becoming happy but not that they have found ultimate happiness. How can they know the entire course of their life during their youth? Although it is only at the end of life that we can say whether a life has been happy or not, it is possible, long before the end of our lives, to participate in our happiness, if we know what our end or purpose is and we are moving toward it.

Happiness as Purpose

Purpose-driven happiness is very different from the contemporary notion of happiness as some state of contentment or pleasure that anyone with enough material resources can realize. The contemporary notion would have us believe that since young people in many Western industrialized nations have access to limitless resources, they should be among the happiest people in the world. Of course, that is not what we find, since all of the physical pleasure and contentment in the world cannot make up for a lack of purpose and direction in our lives. Unless we can integrate our pleasure with our ultimate goal or end, we will not find happiness. In our culture, young people are told that they are experiencing the happiest time of their lives, but they are given little or no direction. No wonder that suicide rates are so high among them.

Youth is difficult because human beings are not automatically assigned a *telos* or ultimate goal, and thus they do not naturally move toward established ends the way the rest of nature does. We are not like acorns that all move instinctively toward the same end. Aside from a general hierarchy of needs, we have little in the way of natural pointers or indicators for our life's direction. Perhaps the only thing that human nature provides is a general recognition that we desire a purpose but lack any knowledge of what would constitute that specific purpose.

Immanuel Kant had claimed that, unlike the rest of nature for which their *telos* is a given, our *telos* of human happiness is not naturally provided and requires both consciousness and choice on our part.

Nature has willed that man shall produce wholly out of himself all that goes beyond the mechanical structure and arrangement of his animal existence, and that he shall participate in no other happiness or perfection [than that which] he has procured for himself, apart from instinct, by his own Reason.[4]

Kant goes on to say that nature has given human beings "reason and freedom of will"[5] from which human beings must choose for themselves the ends that will constitute their happiness. This certainly seems to be the case. Even the most unreflective person ponders his or her own personal happiness and how it could be achieved.

The Modern Undermining of Happiness

Unfortunately, forces at work throughout the modern period have undermined our efforts to find the ends that constitute our happiness. Although Kant utilized Aristotle's view, most key figures of the modern period replaced Aristotle's biological view of the universe with a mechanical view. Accordingly, things were not perceived to move in conformity to their ends. Rather, they were thought to move because of mechanical structures that serve as efficient causes. In a Newtonian world, things move, not because of an attraction toward their end, but because internal structures impel them (but not necessarily in any specific direction). An automobile is a self-mover, but where it moves is not determined by its mechanical structure. We, the drivers, and not the automobile, decide where it will go.

Add the Darwinian notion of change to the modernist mechanical view and it becomes even more difficult to discover our purpose. The Darwinian view perceived changes to species as random and completely without purpose. According to Darwin, characteristics are adapted into species because they happen to be conducive to procreation and thus successive generations end up with those characteristics. There is no plan or purpose to these changes. Mutations simply occur, and some turn out to be advantageous; others are detrimental. Thus, a major effect of Darwinian science was to offer an explanation of our origin without any plan or intention, that is, without teleology or purpose.

The advance of urban industrial society has also had a hand in undermining the teleological view, especially in regard to human happiness. With modern, urban society, our occupation is not determined by tradition or inherited from our ancestors, nor is our spouse determined by proximity to our homes. Instead, we are free to choose from thousands of occupations, and we no longer have to marry the girl or boy next door. We can marry someone from another town or another hemisphere. With such freedom, how could only one path represent our true *telos* or happiness?

Despite all this, however, our conversion to the Christian life brings an awareness of a teleological alternative to the freedom of modernity. Indeed, with Christianity, even if we are free from any *given* direction, that does not mean that we must settle for a momentary happiness that is not teleological. Happiness, for the Christian, lies in our awareness that God has a unique plan and purpose for our lives. *For surely I know the plans I have for you, says the* LORD, *plans for your welfare and not for harm, to give you a future with hope* (Jeremiah 29:11).

But what is God's plan for my life? What is the future he has for me? I need to know my end or happiness so that I can move toward and participate in it.

The Great Commission

Of all the things that Jesus instructs us to do, almost all are situated in the present tense. That is, he instructs us concerning an action we should do *now*, or some attitude we should have *now*. He tells us *"Come to me"* (Matthew 11:28), and *"Do not let your hearts be troubled"* (John 14:1), or *"love the Lord your God with all your heart, and with all your soul, and with all your mind"* (Matthew 22:37). All of these are immediate and do not address the future. The only command that Jesus gives that is not immediate seems to be the great commission in which he tells us to *"Go therefore and make disciples of all nations"* (Matthew 28:19) or *"Go into all the world and proclaim the good news"* (Mark 16:15). Since we have not yet made disciples of all the nations, the imperative appears to be intended for the future. Jesus' commission summarizes our end and the happiness we are to seek.

In attempting to understand what it means to "make disciples of all nations," Jesus tells us that we are to teach *"them to obey everything that [he has] commanded [us]"* (Matthew 28:20). But what has he commanded us? Historically, we teach the nations our theological doctrines and religious rituals, but Jesus taught neither. By word and example, Jesus taught us how to have a relationship with God, just as he had a relationship with his Father. Our great commission, then, is to have a relationship with our heavenly Father, just as Jesus does, and to teach others how to do the same.

When we come to Jesus, we learn to experience God's presence, as well as the joy and peace that it brings, but we often still lack a sense of happiness or purpose. Such happiness is not easily realized. God calls each Christian in a unique way. Just as we each have a unique relationship with God, so too do we have a unique purpose. The fullness of the gospel is not simply to know God, but to be disciples and teach others to also know him. This is the great commission—the fullness of our happiness. Such happiness is not easily realized. God calls each Christian in a unique way, and just as we each have a unique relationship with God, so too do we each have a unique purpose or way to share that relationship with others. This is the great challenge to our happiness. Will we be able to discover the unique way that God intends us to fulfill the great commission? We may know that we are to go and make disciples, but do we understand how to do it, and what that uniquely means for us? We are all faced with this challenge.

Realizing Our Happiness

Many young Christians have deep and dynamic relationships with God. They know God, but they are not so sure about who they are and where they are going. Many people never realize their unique potential to lead others to know God just as they have come to know him. They may experience God's presence, but without discovering the unique way they are to fulfill the great commission, they will never experience the happiness that only comes from knowing the end for which they were uniquely created. In the absence of such knowledge, true happiness eludes them, and they settle for whatever their culture suggests.

Sadly, when they look to the modern Church community, they often find little comfort. We tell young Christians that God has a very special plan for their lives, a special way for them to realize the great commission, and then we demand that they conform and be like everyone else. We teach them about the objective truth of Christianity, but they desperately need to know what God has particularly for them. We give them instruction so they can teach like others teach or write like others write, but we do not give them instruction concerning the unique ministry and end God has just for them. They desperately need personal mentors who can facilitate their understanding of God's commission for their particular lives.

Of course, many older Christians are not well suited to meet such a need since they themselves have succumbed to the cultural pressure of believing that happiness is related to wealth or status. Most of us seek happiness in the same place as everyone else, but the only way to find the real happiness we seek—that deep happiness that goes to the core of our being—is by discovering and pursuing the end for which we were created. To simply know God is not an end. It is a moment of peace and joy, but not an end. In order to come into the fullness of life that Jesus promises, we need more than peace and joy. We need happiness, and true happiness only comes when we realize and pursue the unique way God desires for us to spread the Good News.

God is faithful to reveal our unique happiness, if we reject the temptation to accept a cultural notion of happiness and continue to seek our happiness in the great commission. To succeed in this Christian journey and come into the fullness of life that God has in store for us, we must keep our eye fixed upon the unique end that God has set before us.

I remember hearing a story about a marathon swimmer who was trying to swim from Catalina Island to the California coast (about thirty miles). It was a very cold day with a heavy fog. The swim was unsuccessful and the woman was pulled from the water a mile short of the coast. The sportswriters who were interviewing her assumed that the cold water was what undermined her effort, but when questioned, she claimed that it was not the cold that brought the swim to an end short of the goal but the fog. The sportswriters were puzzled by her response. They could understand how the cold could have affected her, but how was the fog a factor? She then explained, "If I could have seen the coast, I would have made it."

Like that swimmer, we need to see our end. We need to know the purpose for which we were created—the reason we came into the world.

We need to know how we were uniquely made to fulfill the great commission. This is the ultimate revelation that constitutes our happiness.

Questions for Reflection

1. What is happiness?
2. How is happiness related to our Christian purpose in life?
3. What impact did modernism (including Darwinisn and the Industrial Revolution) have on our perception of purpose and happiness?
4. What is our *commission,* and how is it related to happiness?

13

Conclusion: Subjective Theology as Dialogue With God

This chapter provides a summary explanation for the kind of theology we have been developing throughout these chapters. Specifically, it focuses on the nature of those concepts that lie at the base of our theology and how they might be communicated to us by God.

Clearly, God's concepts are not our concepts. For one thing, God's concepts are not common or the product of a human language community. Ludwig Wittgenstein had argued that there could be no such thing as a private language with words that refer to concepts or inner experiences that are totally private and known only to an individual.[1] The Trinity constitutes a community, so to speak, but a divine community is very different from a limited human language community. In the first place, the persons of the Godhead perceive things from the perspective of eternity. Therefore, God's concepts (if we could even call them that) are well beyond the realm of human imagination. This fact alone seems to make it impossible for God to communicate his concepts to us. Even though it is impossible for us to see things from God's perspective, God became human to teach us how we should conceive of God and our relationship with him.

The concepts that comprise Jesus' perspective, and what he is trying to communicate to us, are very different from what Wittgenstein and most others would consider normal human concepts. As we learned at the outset of this book, Jesus' concepts are radically different than those of his language community. Therefore, we wonder if such concepts could be communicated at all, particularly since they are neither common nor the product of a human community. I believe that such concepts can be communicated. My reason is that we, too, have concepts that are very different from those of our language community. Indeed, in addition to the concepts given to us by our language communities, we also have concepts that originate within us.

Personal Concepts

Like Jesus, we possess concepts known only to ourselves. This is not to say that these concepts constitute a private language, but we possess concepts that are personal and not common or the product of a community. In fact, our first concepts were, for the most part, personal concepts. Our initial concept of a dog may have been that of a four-legged house pet that eats socks. As we experienced more instances signified by the word *dog*, our concept changed. Not all instances signified by the word *dog* ate socks, and there were other four-legged house pets that were not dogs. With these additional experiences, our concept was molded into the common concept, but it began as a personal or private one.

Additionally, we retain many concepts that are not the products of our language communities but are the result of our own personal experience and judgment. For example, in addition to my common concept of *water* or the more scientific concept known as H_2O, I also have a concept of water as the stuff I swam in as a child who spent his summers in a bathing suit and was constantly in the water. My personal concept is very different from the general concept held by my language community. It is a private concept of water that has a unique meaning for me. I do not commonly communicate this concept of water, but it is a concept I am able to and may wish to communicate in my more intimate interactions.

An accepted concept for a language community is little more than a shared linguistic boundary that separates one kind of thing from another. A personal concept, on the other hand, is really not common at all, nor is it a boundary. Many people today still think of general concepts as ideal forms, the true essence of a thing. This is similar to Plato's idea of a concept, where *eidos* (ideal forms) produce a common understanding by uniting members of a species under a certain abstract idea.[2] Personal concepts differ from Platonic forms in that they are not for the purpose of creating a common understanding, nor are they known in abstract objectivity. Personal concepts reflect the unique perspective of an individual.

In common communication, we use concepts for the purpose of utility, and thus knowing the intentional meaning of a speaker is not important. However, at other times, such as when we wish to communicate for the purpose of intimacy, the intentional meaning or personal concept of the speaker is what we seek. We must look beyond general concepts in order to acquire deeper and richer relationships with others.

Common concepts, since they are mainly for the purpose of utility, are simply a means to identify the extensions or instances to which a concept refers. With our personal concepts, however, the instances or extensions of the concept are the means, and the purpose is to communicate the concept itself. Of course, an exact communication of such an intentional meaning is impossible. The purpose of personal communication, however, is not to establish the kind of exactness sought by science, but to intimately share with another person the way we uniquely conceptualize the world.

Personal concepts may begin as common concepts acquired through language, but because they become concepts that are of particular interest and importance to us, we attach additional meaning and significance to them. Such concepts often define us more than our occupations or social statuses, and such concepts often represent the objects of our greatest interest and affection. The woman who loves dogs has a very different concept of dogs than other members of the language community. She is familiar with the common concept, but her personal concept includes things that the one who is not a dog lover would have difficulty imagining. Similarly, a lover of money has a concept of *money* that goes far beyond the concept others signify by the same word. More than our fingerprints, our personal concepts define us because of the time and attention we have devoted to them. These are the things we share in our most intimate relationships, and these are the things we are often most attracted to in other people.

The way in which personal concepts are communicated is very similar to the way common concepts are communicated to us in our initial exposure to language. As we learned previously, a child's concept of a dog may begin as something very different from that of their language community. However, the concept is shaped as additional instances of the signifier or word *dog* are provided. With additional instances, eventually a child's concept becomes something close to the concept held by the language community at large. Likewise, the same is true regarding the communication of our private concepts. The difference lies in the fact that with the communication of private concepts, there is a single instructor concerning the correct extension of the concept, and those extensions include many aspects unique to one's personal experiences, judgments, and values. These unique aspects of the concept are not part of the public version of the same signifier or word. The other main difference lies in the previously mentioned fact that the purpose of communicating a personal concept is to be more intimately known by another person.

Knowing Personal Concepts

In order to know the personal concepts of another person, either human or divine, three things must be considered. The first is natural estrangement. That is, if these concepts are important to the other person, they will most likely be different than the general concept of the language community. Thus, whatever effort we make to understand the personal nature of those concepts is better than supposing that their concept must be like our own. Second, since the object of our knowledge is a person, such knowledge will never be final but must remain open to revision. Knowledge, especially the knowledge of another person (human or divine) is a quest and not an achievable end. It is like the stars, which, although never reached, provide sailors with markers to set their course. Finally, our understanding of such concepts will never approach the kind of exactness we find in mathematics. Personal concepts are broad and multifarious. They are therefore very distinct from the kind of narrow, precise mathematical concepts that were idealized by the science of modernity.

With these caveats in mind, it is possible to know the personal concepts of another person, although the means to such knowledge will be very different from what modernity had set forth as the means to knowledge in general. The primary means to know private concepts is dialogue. Questioning is essential to any dialogue. Through dialogue the interlocutor opens herself or himself to receive the personal concepts of another person. That is, the person to whom the concept is being communicated must also participate, and this participation essentially amounts to asking questions. In short, it is only by questioning that we remain open to receiving the other person's unique conceptual understanding.

> As the art of asking questions, dialectic proves its value because only the person who knows how to ask questions is able to persist in his questioning, which involves being able to preserve his orientation toward openness.[3]

The rules for dialogue are no less true when communicating with God. We must participate in God's revelation by formulating the next question that opens us to further revelations. Of course, the understanding we derive from this questioning and openness will never amount to a comprehensive understanding. We may gain particular insights about people or God, but we can never completely overcome the mystery of others. We do, however, achieve a deeper intimacy with them. The great error to which we so easily succumb is to either believe that another person is not knowable, or to believe that they are completely knowable. Our understanding of God, like our understanding of anyone with whom we are intimate, is both something we grasp and something that escapes our grasp.

Our Knowledge of God and His Concepts

Many Christians claim to have a personal relationship with Jesus. Any genuinely intimate relationship should teach us something of the other person's most important personal concepts. Similarly, if we admire, or even claim to worship, others, we should desire to make some of their personal concepts our own. Of course, in our relationship with Jesus, we need to remember, as we have repeatedly noted, that our understanding will never exactly replicate his. Although over time we may gain insight and take on more of Jesus' perspective, our understanding of him will always be limited by our all-too-human concepts.

Faced with this reality of personal concepts and the fact that they can never be exactly communicated, how do we formulate correct doctrines? The theorists of the past may have been able to naively suppose that, since God's word was inerrant, so was the meaning that we attributed to those words. Since it is no longer possible to maintain such *naiveté*, how are we to create doctrines that we purport to be true?

First, we need to understand that despite all the factors that render our understanding perspectival and relative, our understanding is not relative in the sense that we can think anything we want. If we truly are in an ongoing dialogue, we will be anchored from drifting too far. Just as the external world of sense data provides an anchor for our understanding of the physical world, the other person in a dialogue provides an anchor that keeps us from thinking anything we want about that person. That other person, in fact, provides much more of an anchor than the sense data of the physical world. With the physical world, we are at great liberty to conceptualize data, not in any way we want, but in a great variety of ways. Such freedom is more limited in a dialogue that seeks to know another person. The other person prevents us from believing a vast variety of false assumptions. If we allow our questions to keep us open to their understanding, and the other person is trustworthy and forthright, our understanding of them will constantly be kept in check and not allowed to drift too far from the reality of what that person is trying to communicate. Thus, although the thing we seek to know is not an object but a subject, and our knowledge will be subjective rather than objective, our understanding is not wildly relative. As long as we stay in dialogue and allow that other person or their text to continually correct our understanding, we will be brought into an ever-greater personal knowledge and intimacy.

This ongoing dialogue, when it is with the persons of the Christian Godhead, also provides us with a knowledge that is certain. Of course, the certainty we have concerning that knowledge is unlike the objective certainty of mathematics. The certainty we acquire through our ongoing dialogue with God is a subjective certainty concerning God's faithfulness. Subjective certainty develops slowly over time as another person consistently demonstrates their faithfulness to us. This subjective certainty is also different from the kind of certainty we find in mathematics in that it is not a certainty that we can demonstrate to others. When God is repeatedly faithful and trustworthy, we cannot demonstrate his fidelity with scientific certitude. Others may see fruit in our lives, but the source of that fruitfulness cannot be seen. Our experiences of God's faithfulness cannot be transferred to another in order to serve as the basis of their faith. In our relationships with God, we must gain confidence and certainty through our own personal encounter and experience.

This kind of subjective, relative, and certain understanding of God is more conducive to the spirit of Christianity than the objective and universal understanding that theologians of the past attempted to set forth. To begin with, it produces an invaluable humility in us. With the view we have been suggesting, whatever our theology, we never have the last word. Our understanding of God is always ongoing and therefore never final. We desire finality and a theology that purports to be objective seems to give us what we want. Objective and universal theology is attractive because it puts us in charge, whereas a theology based on an ongoing dialogue puts God in charge and reduces us to our proper place of humility and dependence.

The consequence of such humility and dependence is that it causes us to draw near to God and to seek his wisdom rather than depending on our own. Admittedly, such dependence is uncomfortable, and we prefer to have more knowledge of God so that we can serve him out of our own knowledge and ability rather than out of a dependence on his wisdom and grace. However, the gospels teach us that a dependent relationship with God is the very essence of the Christian life.

God could have equipped us with a more adequate understanding based on more divine concepts. The fact that he has not chosen to give us these tools tells us that such a situation would not be ideal. Instead, God has done something better. God chose to retain true knowledge for himself and dispense wisdom as individuals sought his counsel. This is a central theme of the gospel. Jesus commands us to follow him and to live as he lived. The way he lived was to be in constant communion (that is, dialogic communication) with the Father, and to do nothing apart from that communion.

"The Son can do nothing on his own, but only what he sees the Father doing; for whatever the Father does, the Son does likewise" (John 5:19).

"The words that I say to you I do not speak on my own; but the Father who dwells in me does his works" (John 14:10).

God desires that we live close enough to him to be guided by his wisdom rather than our own. We have access to true wisdom, but it is not granted through objective methods like those of mathematics and science but through a personal relationship with the living God. This is why, in both the third chapter of James' Epistle and the second and third chapters of 1 Corinthians, we are told that there are *two* wisdoms. One is a wisdom that *does not come down from above, but is earthly...* (James 3:15), and another is wisdom that comes from heaven—*a wisdom from above* (James 3:17). If our theology is to be based on a wisdom that comes down from heaven, it must be a theology rooted in a personal and intimate dialogue with God. It must be rooted, not in the narrow and exacting doctrines that we create out of our desire for something that we can get a hold of, but on an ongoing dialogic relationship in which God gets a hold of us.

The Consequence of a Subjective Theology

It will only be through such a dialogic communication, and the subjective and perspectivally relative theology it produces, that we will achieve the kind of unity that God intends for his people. What has kept Christians apart for so long has been the belief that an objective and universal theology was possible. Once constructed, such an objective theology causes us to be prejudiced against anyone with a different perspective. In the past, Christians have killed one another over doctrinal points because they believed they were in possession of an objective and universal truth.

Such a position is not possible if we believe that our understanding of God comes through a dialogue that is personal, intimate, and ongoing. With such a view, it is easy to understand how others can be in different places along the Christian journey. Indeed, the same Scripture and the same God have different meaning to a seven-year-old who has just encountered God for the first time than for a person who has been on the journey for decades. True, the seven-year-old can experience God every bit as much as the mature Christian, but the child's understanding and the meaning attributed to that experience will certainly be different. The greatest difference between the two is that the new believer is tempted to think that his or her understanding is complete, whereas the mature believer can no longer draw such a conclusion. Unfortunately, this is not always the case. Often, older Christians become proud of their understanding and rigid in their beliefs, and thus they do not accept their humble calling. Often their idea of God has narrowed rather than broadened, and their doctrines have become more limiting. Such a theology is the product of the ego's desire for objective certainty rather than genuine communion with God.

A mature believer whose wisdom has come down from above (see James 3:17) and whose theology is the result of an ongoing, dialogic journey, is much different. Such a believer is more likely to embrace what a colleague of mine refers to as *humble hermeneutics*. Humble hermeneutics results from a reduced confidence in our own understanding, and it allows us to recognize that other human beings, even those very different from ourselves, are equally engaged in this mysterious journey that is the Christian life.

Of course, this does not mean that we are not to seek truth, especially the truth of the important concepts that lie at the base of our theological understanding. In that dialogic process toward truth, however, we can never lose sight of the fact that it is still *our* concepts that are produced through communion with God. That is, despite the fact that we are in communion with God, we have no receptors that are not filtered by our fallible, human understanding.

Questions for Reflection

1. What does it mean to have a personal relationship with God? Or with another person?
2. What three things can help us become more intimate with God?
3. How can humility and dependence set us free?

Notes

Introduction

1. Hans-Georg Gadamer, *Philosophical Hermeneutics,* trans. and ed. David Linge (Berkeley, CA: University of California Press, 1976), 9.
2. I would especially like to thank Danny Michaels, my editor at Liguori. His very substantial contribution has greatly enhanced this work, and I am grateful for the effort and talent he brought to this project.

Chapter 1

1. Merold E. Westphal, *Overcoming Onto-Theology: Toward a Postmodern Christian Faith* (New York: Fordham University Press, 2001), 86.
2. Kenell Touryan, "Are Truth Claims in Science Socially Constructed?" *Perspectives on Science and Christian Faith* June (1999): 103.
3. René Descartes, "Discourse on the Method," in *Philosophical Works of Descartes,* vol. 1, trans. Elizabeth S. Haldane and G.R.T. Ross (New York: Dover Publications, 1955), 92.
4. Ibid.
5. Ibid.
6. Ibid.
7. Plato, "Euthydemus," in *The Collected Dialogues of Plato,* trans. W.H.D. Rouse, eds. Edith Hamilton and Huntington Cairns (Princeton, NJ: Princeton University Press, 1989), 385–420.
8. Descartes, 120.
9. Ibid.
10. Ibid., 92.
11. Augustine, *The Confessions of Saint Augustine,* trans. Edward B. Pusey (New York: Washington Square Press, 1962), 308.

12. Ibid., 301.
13. Ibid.
14. Westphal, 189.
15. Westphal, 65.
16. Ibid., 84.
17. William James, *The Will to Believe/Human Immortality and Other Essays in Popular Philosophy* (New York: Dover Publications, Inc., 1956), 28.
18. Aldous Huxley, *The Doors of Perception & Heaven and Hell* (New York: Harper & Brothers Publishers, 1956), 79.

Chapter 2

1. James P. Danaher, "The Dynamics of Faith: From Hope to Knowledge," *Asbury Theological Journal*, 55, no. 2 (Fall 2000), 75–84.

Chapter 3

1. Aristotle, "Nicomachean Ethic," in *The Basic Works of Aristotle,* ed. Richard Mckeon (New York: Random House, 1941), 1178b:8–32.
2. Ibid., "Metaphysics," 1074b.
3. John Piper, *God's Passion for His Glory* (Wheaton, IL: Crossway Books, 1998), 32.
4. Jonathan Edwards, "The End for Which God Created the World," in *God's Passion for His Glory,* ed. John Piper (Wheaton, IL: Crossway Books, 1998), 176.
5. Elizabeth Dreyer, *Passionate Spirituality* (Mahwah, NJ: Paulist Press, 2005), 56–57.
6. Bernard of Clairvaux, *On the Song of Songs,* Vol. III, Sermon 61.2 (Kalamazoo, MI: Cistercian Publications, 1979), 14.
7. José Ortega y Gasset, *On Love: Aspects of a Single Theme,* trans. Toby Talbot (New York: Penguin Books, 1957), 64.
8. Ibid., 65.
9. Ibid., 62–63.

Chapter 4

1. François de Salignac de La Mothe Fénelon, *The Seeking Heart* (Sargent, GA: Seedsowers, 1992), 143.

Chapter 6

1. Michael Casey, *Fully Human, Fully Divine: An Interactive Christology* (Liguori, MO: Liguori Publications, 2004).
2. Westphal, 79.
3. Ibid., 80.

Chapter 7

1. Anselm of Canterbury, *The Major Works,* eds. Brian Davies and G.R. Evans (New York: Oxford University Press, 1998), 272.
2. Ibid.
3. J. Denny Weaver, "Violence in Christian Theology," *Cross Currents* 51, no. 2 (2001): 151.
4. Ibid., 152.
5. J. Patout Burns, "The Concept of Satisfaction in Medieval Redemption Theory," *Theological Studies* 36 (1975): 290.
6. John Mark Hicks, "What Did Christ Accomplish on the Cross? Atonement in Campbell, Stone, and Scott," *Lexington Theological Quarterly* 30, Fall (1995): 154.
7. Ibid., 145-146.
8. David M. Gustafson, "J. G. Princell and the Waldenstromian View of the Atonement," *Trinity Journal* 20, no. 2 (1999): 192.
9. Nancy J. Duff, "Atonement and the Christian Life," *Interpretations* 53, no. 1 (1999): 30.
10. William Placher, "Christ Takes Our Place: Rethinking Atonement," *Interpretations* 53, no. 1 (1999): 11.

Chapter 8

1. Aristotle, "Categories," in *The Basic Works of Aristotle,* ed. Richard Mckeon (New York: Random House, 1941), 2a34.
2. Aristotle, "Metaphysics," 1028a31-1028a35.
3. John S. Mbiti, *African Religions and Philosophy* (London: Heinemann, 1969), 214.
4. Thomas Aquinas, "Summa Theologica," in *Basic Writings of St. Thomas Aquinas,* vol. 1, ed. Anton C. Pegis (New York: Random House, 1945), 1:29,4.
5. Catherine Mowry LaCugna, *God for Us: The Trinity and Christian Life* (San Francisco: Harper Collins, 1991), 271.
6. Ibid., 270–71.
7. Ibid., 272.
8. Reprinted in LaCugna, 275.

Chapter 9

1. Plato, "Phaedo," in *The Collected Dialogues of Plato,* trans. Hugh Tredennick, eds. Edith Hamilton and Huntington Cairns (Princeton, NJ: Princeton University Press, 1989), 65 c–d.
2. William Shakespeare, *Hamlet,* Act 3, sc. 1.

Chapter 10

1. Michael O'Neil, "Karl Barth's Doctrine of Election," *Evangelical Quarterly* 76, no. 4 (2004), 322.

Chapter 11

1. James, 25.
2. Andrew M. Greeley, "The Apologetics of Beauty" *America* 183, no. 7 (2000): 3.
3. Aidan Nichols, "Von Balthasar's Aim in His Theological Aesthetic," *The Heythrop Journal* 40 (1999): 410.
4. James, 17.
5. Ibid., 30.

Chapter 12

1. Aristotle, *Nicomachean Ethic*, 1097b 21–22.
2. Ibid., 1098a 18–19.
3. Ibid., 1100a 1–2.
4. Immanuel Kant, "Idea of a Universal History from a Cosmopolitan Point of View," in *Theories of History: Readings from Classical and Contemporary Sources*, ed. Patrick Gardiner (New York: The Free Press, 1959), 24.
5. Ibid.

Chapter 13

1. Ludwig Wittgenstein, *Philosophical Investigations*, trans. G.E.M. Anscombe (New York: MacMillan Publishing Co. Inc., 1968), secs. 243–315.
2. Plato, "Meno," in *Plato: Collected Dialogues*, trans. Hugh Tredennick, eds. Edith Hamilton and Huntington Cairns (Princeton, NJ: Princeton University Press, 1989), 72–79.
3. Hans-Georg Gadamer, *Truth and Method*, trans. Joel Weinsheimer and Donald G. Marshall (New York: Continuum Publishing, 1999), 367.

Works Cited

Anselm of Canterbury. *Anselm of Canterbury: The Major Works*. Edited by Brian Davies and Gill R. Evans. New York: Oxford University Press, 1998.

Aquinas, Thomas. *Summa Theologica. Basic Writings of St. Thomas Aquinas*, vol. 1. Edited by Anton C. Pegis. New York: Random House, 1945.

Aristotle. "Categories," in *The Basic Works of Aristotle*. Edited by Richard Mckeon. New York: Random House, 1941.

———. "Metaphysics," in *The Basic Works of Aristotle*. Edited by Richard Mckeon. New York: Random House, 1941.

———. "Nicomachean Ethic," in *The Basic Works of Aristotle*. Edited by Richard Mckeon. New York: Random House, 1941.

Augustine, *The Confessions of Saint Augustine*. Translated by Edward B. Pusey. New York: Washington Square Press, 1962.

Burns, J. Patout. "The Concept of Satisfaction in Medieval Redemption Theory." *Theological Studies* 36 (1975): 290.

Descartes, Réne. "Discourse on the Method," in *Philosophical Works of Descartes*, vol. 1. Translated by Elizabeth S. Haldane and G.R.T. Ross. New York: Dover Publications, 1955.

Dreyer, Elizabeth. *Passionate Spirituality*. Mahwah, NJ: Paulist Press, 2005.

Duff, Nancy J. "Atonement and the Christian Life." *Interpretations* 53, no. 1 (1999): 30.

Edwards, Jonathan. *The End for Which God Created the World. God's Passion for His Glory*. Edited by John Piper. Wheaton, IL: Crossway Books, 1998.

Fénelon, François de Salignac de La Monthe. *The Seeking Heart*. Sargent, GA: Seedsowers, 1992.

Gadamer, Hans-Georg. *Truth and Method*. Translated by Joel Weinsheimer and Donald G. Marshall. New York: Continuum Publishing, 1999.

Greeley, Andrew M. "The Apologetics of Beauty." *America* 183, no. 7 (2000): 8.

Gustafson, David M. "J. G. Princell and the Waldenstromian View of the Atonement." *Trinity Journal* 20 no. 2 (1999): 192.

Hicks, John Mark. "What Did Christ Accomplish on the Cross? Atonement in Campbell, Stone, and Scott." *Lexington Theological Quarterly* 30, Fall (1995): 154.

Huxley, Aldous. *The Doors of Perception, and Heaven and Hell.* New York: Harper & Row, 1956.

James, William. Quoted in *The Will to Believe/Human Immortality and Other Essays on Popular Philosophy.* New York: Dover Publications, 1956, 1–31.

Johnson, Luke Timothy. *Jesus and the Gospels.* Chantilly, VA: The Teaching Company, 2004.

Kant, Immanuel. "Idea of a Universal History From a Cosmopolitan Point of View," in *Theories of History; Readings From Classical and Contemporary Sources.* Edited by Patrick Gardiner. New York: The Free Press, 1959, 24.

LaCugna, Catherine Mowry. *God for Us: The Trinity and Christian Life.* San Francisco: Harper Collins, 1991.

McLaren, Brian D. *A Generous Orthodoxy.* Grand Rapids, MI: Zondervan, 2004.

Nichols, Aidan. "Von Balthasar's Aim in His Theological Aesthetic." *The Heythrop Journal* 40 (1999): 409–23.

O'Neil, Michael. "Karl Barth's Doctrine of Election." *Evangelical Quarterly* 76, no. 4 (2004): 311–26.

Ortega y Gasset, José. *On Love: Aspects of a Single Theme.* Translated by Toby Talbot. New York: Penguin Books, 1957.

Piper, John. *God's Passion for His Glory.* Wheaton, IL: Crossway Books, 1998, 32.

Placher, William. "Christ Takes Our Place: Rethinking Atonement." *Interpretations* 53, no. 1 (1999): 11.

Plato. "Euthydemus," in *The Collected Dialogues of Plato.* Translated by W.H.D. Rouse; edited by Edith Hamilton and Huntington Cairns. Princeton, NJ: Princeton University Press, 1989, 385–420.

———. "Meno," in *The Collected Dialogues of Plato.* Edited by Edith Hamilton and Huntington Cairns. Princeton, NJ: Princeton University Press, 1989, 72–9.

———"Phaedo," in *The Collected Dialogues of Plato.* Translated by Hugh Tredennick; edited by Edith Hamilton and Huntington Cairns. Princeton, NJ: Princeton University Press, 1989, 526–74.

Prothero, Stephen. *American Jesus.* New York: Farrar, Straus and Giroux, 2003.

Touryan, Kenell. "Are Truth Claims in Science Socially Constructed?" *Perspectives on Science and Christian Faith* 51, June (1999): 102–7.

Weaver, J. Denny. "Violence in Christian Theology." *Cross Currents* 51, no. 2 (2001): 151.

Westphal, Merold E. *Overcoming Onto-Theology: Toward a Postmodern Christian Faith.* New York: Fordham University Press, 2001.

Wittgenstein, Ludwig. *Philosophical Investigations.* Translated by G.E.M. Anscombe. New York: MacMillan Publishing, 1968.

Index